TREASURES OF THE ISRAEL MUSEUM
LES TRÉSORS DU MUSÉE D'ISRAËL
KUNSTSCHÄTZE DES ISRAEL MUSEUMS
אוצרות מוזיאון ישראל

Exhibition poster, 1979

TREASURES
OF THE
ISRAEL MUSEUM
JERUSALEM

SPONSORED BY
CAROLINE AND JOSEPH S. GRUSS

PHOTOGRAPHS
BY
PIERRE-ALAIN FERRAZZINI

2644

ISBN 965-278-030-8

TO MAYOR TEDDY KOLLEK
CREATOR OF THE ISRAEL MUSEUM

CAROLINE AND JOSEPH S. GRUSS

A

The treasures of the Israel Museum are themselves housed in a treasure chest, the Museum complex. Situated on a hill amidst ancient olive trees, overlooking the Knesset, the Hebrew University campus, and the venerable Monastery of the Cross, the Museum has become an architectural landmark. The modular concept of the building, designed by Israeli architects Al Mansfeld and Dora Gad, has enabled the Museum to grow gallery by gallery, pavilion by pavilion. The distinctive dome of the Shrine of the Book, conceived by Armand Bartos and Frederick Kiesler to house the historic Dead Sea Scrolls, has become one of Jerusalem's most familiar structures. The Billy Rose Art Garden, created by Isamu Noguchi, is a majestic setting for modern sculpture.

It is hard to believe that two decades ago, this splendid institution was merely a dream. Teddy Kollek, who became Mayor of Jerusalem shortly after the Museum's opening, was one of a few people who looked beyond the immediate.

The museum he and others envisioned would emphasize the history and tradition of the Land of Israel and the heritage of the Jewish people in the Diaspora and, at the same time, display the best of human creativity of all ages.

The expectations – even of the dreamers – were modest, expectations belied by the reality of today. The growth of the Museum, the nearly one million visitors each year, its cultural and educational focus, the international renown it has achieved, have surpassed even fantasy.

From its very beginning, there was a basic tenet which has guided the Museum throughout the years: high standards, an insistence on quality and selectivity, a motif imbued by the late Willem Sandberg, the first Art Advisor to the Israel Museum.

There was no definitive framework for the growth of the Museum collections. Some expanded naturally: the galleries of local archaeology through archaeological excavations in Israel. The collections of ancient Near Eastern art grew mainly through gifts; ethnography, painstakingly, through surveys and studies and even excavating from under mattresses the relics and remnants which immigrants carried with them to Israel from every country; Judaica, by the addition of priceless treasures; Israeli art, by a more systematic approach and the help of both collectors and artists; design, through contact with the contemporary world of technology and industry; modern art, photography, primitive arts, the Far East, period rooms – collections developed and expanded through the untiring efforts of our friends.

The Museum's permanent collections tell only a partial story. The temporary exhibitions – ranging from prehistory to contemporary industrial concepts – educate and enlighten and entertain. They widen the horizons of a public with diverse roots in four continents living in a country geographically isolated.

It is a museum for the past and for the present – but very much for the future. The Museum's youth wing is one of the largest, most innovative and most well known facility of its kind. It opens up untold new worlds for our children and has become an important tool for the integration of youngsters of different backgrounds.

From the Museum's early beginnings, Caroline and Joseph Gruss of New York – who combined a deep conviction of the importance of the preservation of the Jewish heritage with a true love of art and elegant taste – shared our dreams. They had a special understanding of the Museum's needs and their help has ranged from the creation of the Memorial Room for Jewish Artists Who Perished in the Holocaust, to the sponsorship of the Caroline and Joseph Gruss Gallery for Israeli Art, and the support of the Judaica Department. Mr. and Mrs. Gruss not only undertook the publication of this beautiful volume, it was in fact they who conceived the idea as a celebration of the Museum's 20th anniversary. For all they have done for us – and for their belief in what we could do – we thank them.

Dr. Martin WEYL, Director

B

Parmi des oliviers plus que centenaires, sur une colline ayant vue sur la Knesset, le campus de l'Université Hébraïque et la Vallée de la Croix, le Musée d'Israël impose son complexe architectural dans le panorama de Jérusalem. La conception modulaire de l'ensemble, due aux architectes israéliens Al Mansfeld et Dora Gad, a permis l'expansion du Musée selon ses besoins, étape par étape, salle par salle. Le dôme du Sanctuaire du Livre, conçu par Armand Bartos et Frederick Kiesler pour la présentation des fameux Manuscrits de la mer Morte, est devenu l'un des édifices les plus familiers dans le paysage. La sculpture moderne, enfin, a trouvé un cadre majestueux dans le Jardin Billy Rose, créé par Isamu Noguchi.

Il est difficile de croire qu'il y a à peine deux décennies cette réalisation n'était encore qu'un rêve. Teddy Kollek, élu maire de Jérusalem peu après l'inauguration du Musée, fut l'une des rares personnes qui envisagèrent une institution qui réunirait la culture et les traditions de la terre d'Israël et le patrimoine du peuple juif dans la Diaspora, et présenterait parallèlement le meilleur de ce que l'homme a créé à travers les temps.

Les espérances d'alors sont bien dépassées par la réalité d'aujourd'hui. L'expansion du Musée, le nombre important de visiteurs – près d'un million par an – les activités culturelles et éducatives, la réputation qu'il a acquise dans le monde, vont au-delà même des fantaisies les plus audacieuses. Dès le début, la règle fondamentale, inspirée par le premier conseiller artistique du Musée d'Israël, le regretté Willem Sandberg, a été le maintien d'un haut niveau et le discernement dans le choix et la qualité des acquisitions.

Il n'y avait toutefois au départ aucun programme d'acquisitions arrêté. Certaines collections se sont agrandies tout naturellement. Les salles consacrées à l'archéologie locale, par exemple, reflètent les résultats des fouilles entreprises en Israël, tandis que les collections du Proche-Orient ancien se sont créées surtout grâce à des dons. Le département d'Ethnographie s'est développé, non sans peine, à la suite de recherches et d'enquêtes allant jusqu'à la découverte sous les matelas des reliques et des fragments du passé apportés par les immigrants de tous pays. La Judaïca s'est enrichie de trésors inestimables. La collection d'art israélien est née avec l'aide des artistes eux-mêmes et des collectionneurs. L'art moderne, le design, la photographie, les arts primitifs et d'Extrême-Orient, les salles du XVIIIe siècle ont complété l'ensemble de nos collections grâce aux efforts infatigables de nos amis.

Mais les collections permanentes ne donnent qu'une image imparfaite du Musée. En effet, des expositions temporaires de tous genres – depuis la préhistoire jusqu'à l'esthétique industrielle contemporaine – se succèdent pour éclairer, éduquer et distraire un public venu de quatre continents vivre dans un pays géographiquement isolé.

Le Musée sert le passé et le présent, mais aussi l'avenir. Le Pavillon des Enfants, l'une des institutions les plus dynamiques et les plus innovatrices dans son genre, est une porte ouverte sur des mondes nouveaux et merveilleux. Pour des jeunes venant de milieux très différents, il joue un rôle important dans leur intégration culturelle et sociale.

Dès les premiers temps du Musée, Caroline et Joseph Gruss de New York, conscients de l'importance de préserver le patrimoine juif et, de plus, amoureux de l'art, ont partagé nos rêves. Ils sentirent d'emblée les besoins du Musée. Leur générosité s'est manifestée de maintes façons, en créant la Salle Commémorative des Artistes Juifs qui ont péri pendant l'Holocauste et la Galerie d'Art israélien, en soutenant le département de la Judaïca, enfin en entreprenant la publication de ce superbe volume pour fêter aujourd'hui le vingtième anniversaire du Musée. Pour tout ce qu'ils ont fait et pour leur foi en notre avenir nous les remercions.

Dr Martin WEYL, Directeur

C

Das Israel Museum, hingestreckt auf einem Hügel zwischen alten Olivenbäumen, mit dem Blick auf das Parlamentsgebäude die «Knesseth», die Hebräische Universität und das ehrwürdige Kreuzkloster, ist zu einem Wahrzeichen Jerusalems geworden. Dieser Gebäudekomplex ist die Schatzkammer, in der die Kostbarkeiten des Israel Museums aufbewahrt werden. Der modulare Plan des Baues, von den israelischen Architekten Al Mansfeld und Dora Gad entworfen, hat dem Museum die Möglichkeit gegeben, sich allmählich, durch jeweiliges Hinzufügen von Galerien und Pavillions, zu entwickeln. Die charakteristische Kuppel des Schreins des Buches, Armand Bartos' und Frederick Kieslers Entwurf, der die historischen Rollen vom Toten Meer beherbergt, gehört zu Jerusalems bekanntesten Baudenkmälern. Der Billy-Rose-Skulpturengarten, das Werk von Isamu Noguchi, bildet einen majestätischen Rahmen für moderne Plastik.

Es ist kaum zu glauben, daß vor nicht mehr als zwanzig Jahren dieses prächtige Museum nur ein Traum war. Teddy Kollek, der kurz nach der Eröffnung des Museums Bürgermeister von Jerusalem wurde, war einer der wenigen, die weit in die Zukunft schauten.

Die wenigen sahen vor ihren Augen ein Museum, das der Geschichte und Tradition des Landes Israel und dem Erbgut des jüdischen Volkes in der Diaspora sichtbaren Ausdruck verleihen würde und gleichzeitig das Beste zeigen sollte, was menschliche Schöpferkraft zu allen Zeiten hervorgebracht hat.

Die Erwartungen – sogar die der Träumer – waren bescheiden, Erwartungen, die die Wirklichkeit von heute Lügen straft. Das Wachstum des Museums, die Zahl der Besucher, die jährlich fast eine Million erreicht, der internationale Ruf, den das Museum sich errungen hat und sein Rang als kultureller und erzieherischer Brennpunkt, haben jede Phantasie übertroffen.

Von Anfang an und durch all die Jahre hindurch wurde das Museum von einem fundamentalen Grundsatz geleitet: hohe Maßstäbe und Beharren auf Qualität waren das Leitmotiv, mit dem der verstorbene Willem Sandberg, der erste Kunstberater des Israel Museums, dem Museum seinen Stempel aufgedrückt hat.

Einen definitiven Rahmen für die Entwicklung der Museums-Sammlungen gab es zunächst nicht. Manche wuchsen auf natürliche Weise. So spiegeln die Galerien für die Archäologie des Landes die archäologischen Ausgrabungen in Israel wider. Die Sammlungen der alten Kunst des nahen Ostens wurden in der Hauptsache durch Schenkungen erweitert. Die Etnographische Abteilung verdankt ihr Wachstum gewissenhaftem Fleiß, sorgfältigen Bestandaufnahmen und Studien, die mitunter mit regelrechten «Ausgrabungen» von Andenken und Überresten verbunden waren, welche die Einwanderer aller Länder nach Israel mitgebracht hatten und unter den Matratzen aufbewahrten. Die Judaica Abteilung wurde durch unschätzbare Kostbarkeiten bereichert. Die Sammlung israelischer Kunst – deren Wachsen systematischer unternommen wurde – erfreute sich der Hilfe von Sammlern und Künstlern. Design – gewann durch Kontakt mit der Welt der Industrie und Technologie. Moderne Kunst, Photographie, primitive Kunst, der ferne Osten, Stil-Zimmer – alles Sammlungen, die sich durch die unermüdlichen Bemühungen unserer Freunde entwickelt und erweitert haben.

Die permanenten Sammlungen des Museums bedeuten jedoch bei weitem nicht alles. Wechselausstellungen, deren Themen von der Frühgeschichte bis zum zeitgenössischen Industrie Produkt reichen, wirken erzieherisch, aufklärend und unterhaltend. Sie erweitern den Horizont eines Publikums, das seine Wurzeln in vier Kontinenten hat und in einem Lande lebt, das geographisch isoliert ist.

Ein Museum für Vergangenheit und Gegenwart – aber in besonderem Maße ein Museum für die Zukunft. Die Jugend Abteilung des Museums die neue Wege geht ist eine der größten, und best bekannten Institutionen ihrer Art. Sie eröffnet unsern Kindern neue Welten und trägt das ihre zur Integrierung Jugendlicher aus verschiedenen Milieus bei.

Caroline und Joseph Gruss, New York, die mit ihrer tiefen Überzeugung von der Bedeutsamkeit der Erhaltung jüdischen Erbguts echte Liebe für Kunst und guten Geschmack verbinden, haben unsere Träume seit den frühen Anfängen des Museums geteilt. Ihr Verständnis für die Bedürfnisse des Museums war von besonderer Art. Ihrer Hilfe verdanken wir den Raum, der dem Andenken an die jüdischen Künstler gewidmet ist, die den Massenmord zum Opfer fielen, die «Caroline und Joseph Gruss Galerie für israelische Kunst» und die ständige Förderung der Judaica Abteilung. Herr und Frau Gruss haben nicht nur die Veröffentlichung dieses schönen Bandes übernommen, sondern sie waren es auch, die die Idee hatten, das Buch zum 20. Geburtstag des Museums erscheinen zu lassen. Für all das, was sie für uns getan haben und für ihren Glauben in unsere Aufgabe, danken wir Ihnen.

Dr. Martin WEYL, Direktor

D

E

אוצרות מוזיאון ישראל שמורים במבנה שהוא עצמו כתיבת-אוצר: הבניין, העומד על גבעה בתוך חורשת זיתים עתיקים וצופה על הכנסת, על קריית-האוניברסיטה ועל עמק המצלבה, הפך להיות ציון-דרך אדריכלי. התפיסה המודולארית של המבנה, אשר עוצב בידי האדריכלים אל מנספלד ודורה גד, מאפשרת למוזיאון לגדול, אולם אחרי אולם, ביתן אחרי ביתן. היכל הספר, שבו אצורות מגילות ים-המלח, על צורת הכיפה המיוחדת שלו בעיצובם של ארמאנד ברטוס ופרדריק קיסלר, הוא מן המבנים המוכרים והבולטים בנוף ירושלים. גן-האמנות ע״ש בילי רוז, פרי תכנונו של האדריכל איסאמו נוגוצ׳י, מהווה תפאורת-רקע מרשימה לאוסף פיסול מודרני.

קשה להאמין שאך לפני שני עשורים היה מפעל חשוב זה בחזקת חלום בלבד. מר טדי קולק, שנבחר לכהן כראש עיריית ירושלים זמן קצר לאחר פתיחת המוזיאון, היה מן האנשים הספורים שראו מעבר לטווח הקרוב.

המוזיאון אשר הוא ואחרים ראו בחזונם עתיד היה להציג את ההיסטוריה והמסורת של ארץ-ישראל לצד מורשת קהילות ישראל בגלויות השונות, וכן את מיטב היצירה האנושית לדורותיה. הציפיות – אפילו של החוזים עצמם – היו צנועות מלכתחילה, אך המציאות הפריכה אותן: גידולו של המוזיאון – על כמעט מיליון המבקרים בו בשנה, הפיכתו למוקד תרבותי וחינוכי, והפרסום הבינלאומי שלו זכה – כל אלה עלו על כל דמיון.

מלכתחילה עמד לרגלי מייסדי המוזיאון עקרון אחד, והוא שהנחה ומנחה אותם עד היום: הקפדה על סטנדרטים גבוהים, על איכות ועל סלקטיביות – עקרון שבו דגל וילם סנדברג המנוח, היועץ האמנותי הראשון של המוזיאון.

לגידולם וצמיחתם של אוספי המוזיאון לא היתה מתכונת אחידה ומוגדרת. הם שהתפתחו באופן טבעי, כגון אולמות הארכיאולוגיה המקומית – באמצעות ממצאי חפירות. אוספי אמנות המזרח הקדמון גדלו בעיקר הודות לתרומות; אוספי האתנוגרפיה צורפו במאמצים שקדניים בעקבות סקרים ומחקרים, שהוליכו לעתים לגילוי אוצרות טמונים במזרנים – שרידי תרבות הולכת וכלה שהביאו עמם עולים מארצות שונות. האוסף לאמנות יהודית צמח בהוספה מתמדת של תשמישי מצווה וקדושה שאין-ערוך להם. האוסף לאמנות ישראלית נבנה בגישה שיטתית יותר ובסיוע אספנים ואמנים כאחד. המחלקה לעיצוב פועלת מתוך מגע הדוק עם מרכזי טכנולוגיה ותעשייה עדכניים. ואילו המחלקות לאמנות בת-זמננו, לצילום, לאמנויות אתניות ושבטיות ולאמנות המזרח הרחוק, וכן החדרים התקופתיים – כל אלה התפתחו והתפשטו תודות למאמציהם הלא-נלאים של ידידי המוזיאון.

אולם אוספי המוזיאון הקבועים מספרים רק חלק מן הסיפור. התערוכות המתחלפות, העוסקות בנושאים שונים, למן הפרהיסטוריה ועד לעידן המחר במחשבים, באות לחנך, להשכיל, ועם זה לבדר. הן מרחיבות את אופקיו של ציבור רבגוני, החי בבידוד גיאוגרפי, בעוד שורשיו נעוצים בארבע יבשות.

מוזיאון ישראל הוא מוזיאון של העבר ושל ההווה, אך לא פחות – של העתיד. אגף הנוער הוא מן הגדולים, החדשניים והמפורסמים בסוגו. הוא פותח בפני ילדי ירושלים עולמות חדשים שלא שוערו, ובו-בזמן הוא כלי חשוב לאינטגרציה בין צעירים יוצאי סביבה ורקע שונים.

מאז ראשיתו של המוזיאון היו קרוליין ויוסף גרוס מניו-יורק שותפים לנו בחלומותינו. הם משלבים באישיותם אמונה עזה בחשיבות שימורה של המורשת היהודית עם אהבת אמת לאמנות וטעם מעודן. הם הוכיחו הבנה והשתתפות בצרכיו של המוזיאון – מהקמת חדר זיכרון לאמנים יהודיים שנספו בשואה ועד לתרומת אולם קרוליין ויוסף גרוס לאמנות ישראלית וסיוע למחלקה לאמנות יהודית. מר גרוס ורעייתו, לא זו בלבד שנטלו על עצמם את הדפסתו של ספר נאה זה, אלא הם שהגו את עצם הרעיון להוציאו לאור – לכבוד מלאות עשרים שנה למוזיאון. על כל אשר עשו למעננו, ועל אמונתם בכוחנו-אנו לעשות – נתונה תודתנו החמה להם.

דר׳ מרטין וייל, מנהל

I

BEFORE THE ISRAELITES

From remote hunters to early farmers and urban Canaanite civilization.
From flint axes to cult objects and luxury products.

AVANT LES ISRAÉLITES

Des chasseurs lointains aux premiers cultivateurs et à la civilisation Cananéenne.
Des haches de silex aux objets cultuels et aux produits de luxe.

VOR DER ISRAELITISCHEN PERIODE

Von den Jägern der Vorzeit zur frühen Landwirtschaft und der urbanen Zivilisation der Kanaaniter.
Vom Faustkeil zum Kultobjekt und Luxusgegenstand.

התקופה הקדם־ישראלית

מציד של נוודים לחקלאות קדומה ועד לתרבות כנענית עירונית. מגרזני צור לחפצי פולחן
ועד למוצרי מותרות.

FLINT HAND AXES
Maayan Baruch, Upper Galilee, Middle and Upper Acheulian period,
250,000 years Before Present, h. 12-16.3 cm

The fine flaking used in the making of the hand axes indicates the
high technology achieved in this early period.

COUPS-DE-POING DE SILEX
Maayan Baruch, Galilée supérieure, acheuléen moyen et inférieur,
250 000 ans avant notre ère, h. 12-16,3 cm

La manière d'écailler le silex pour façonner les haches préhistoriques montre
le stade de technologie avancé atteint à cette époque.

FAUSTKEILE AUS FEUERSTEIN
Ma'ayan Baruch, Obergaliläa, Mittleres und Spätes Acheuléen,
250 000 v. Chr., H. 12-16,3 cm

Der feine Abschlag bei der Herstellung der Handbeile weist auf den hohen
technologischen Stand dieses frühen Zeitalters hin.

אבני־יד מצור

מעין־ברוך. התקופה האשלית התיכונה והעליונה, 250,000 לפני זמננו. ג 12–16.3 ס"מ

הסיתות העדין של אבני־היד הללו מעיד על הרמה הטכנולוגית הגבוהה שאליה הגיע האדם כבר
בתקופה כה קדומה.

BONE ANIMAL CARVING
HaNahal Cave, Mount Carmel, Natufian Culture,
10,500-8,500 BCE, h. 10.5 cm

This fine image of an animal, naturalistically carved on a sickle handle,
may have been used for ritual purposes.

OS D'ANIMAL SCULPTÉ
Grotte de HaNahal, Mont Carmel, culture natuféenne,
10 500-8500 av. l'ère chrétienne, h. 10,5 cm

Cette belle image d'animal sculptée sur une poignée de faucille était sans doute
destinée à un usage cultuel.

KNOCHENSCHNITZEREI, EIN TIER DARSTELLEND
HaNachal Höhle, Karmelgebirge, Natufische Kultur,
10 500-8500 v. Chr., H. 10,5 cm

Naturalistische Darstellung eines Tieres auf den Griff einer Sichel geschnitzt,
die wahrscheinlich zu rituellen Zwecken benutzt wurde.

חיה מגולפת בעצם

מערת הנחל, הר הכרמל, התרבות הנאטופית, 10,500 – 8,500 לפסה"נ, ג 10.5 ס"מ

דמות חיה זו, המגולפת בסגנון נטורליסטי על ידית מגל, שימשה אולי לצורכי פולחן.

POTTERY FEMALE FIGURINE
Netiv Hagedud, near Jericho, Pre-Pottery Neolithic A,
8,000-7,500 BCE, h. 4.2 cm

The figurine, in a seated position, is one of the earliest known examples
of the use of baked clay.

FIGURINE DE FEMME EN TERRE CUITE
Netiv Hagedud, près de Jéricho, néolithique pré-céramique A,
8000-7500 av. l'ère chrétienne, h. 4,2 cm

Cette figurine de femme assise est l'un des exemples les plus anciens que l'on
connaisse de l'utilisation de la terre cuite.

WEIBLICHE FIGUR AUS TON
Netiv Hagedud bei Jericho, Prä-Keramisches Neolithikum A,
8000-7500 v. Chr., H. 4,2 cm

Die in sitzender Stellung ausgeführte Figur ist eines der frühesten Beispiele
für den Gebrauch von gebranntem Ton.

צלמית אשה מטין

נתיב־הגדוד (ליד יריחו). תקופת האבן החדשה הקדם־קרמית א׳, 8,000 – 7,500 לפסה"נ. ג 4.2 ס"מ

צלמית זו של אשה יושבת היא מן הדוגמאות הקדומות ביותר לשימוש בטין צרוף.

STONE MASK
Horvat Duma, Hebron Hills, pre-Pottery Neolithic B,
7,500-6,200 BCE, h. 22.5 cm

This life-size mask is one of a very few specimens which were
found in Southern Judaea only.

MASQUE EN PIERRE
Horvat Duma, collines de Hébron, néolithique pré-céramique B,
7500-6200 av. l'ère chrétienne, h. 22,5 cm

De grandeur nature, ce masque est un exemple fort rare d'un groupe retrouvé
exclusivement dans le sud de la Judée.

MASKE AUS STEIN
Chorvat Duma, Hebron Hügel, Pre-Keramisches Neolithikum B,
7500-6200 v. Chr., H. 22,5 cm

Diese lebensgroße Maske ist eines der seltenen Exemplare, die ausschließlich
in Süd-Judäa gefunden wurden.

מסכת אדם מאבן

חר' דומה, הר חברון, תקופת האבן החדשה הקדם־קרמית ב', 7,500 – 6,200 לפסה"נ
ג 22.5 ס"מ

מסכה זו, בגודל פני אדם, היא ממצא נדיר שכמותו נמצאו רק דוגמאות ספורות, כולן בדרום־יהודה.

POTTERY FEMALE FIGURINE
Horvat Minha, Jordan Valley, Neolithic period, 6th millennium BCE, h. 11 cm
The importance of this figurine, which may have been the image of a fertility goddess,
lies in its seated position, the unique shape of its head and face,
and the red colour covering the entire piece.

FIGURINE DE FEMME EN TERRE CUITE
Horvat Minha, vallée du Jourdain, période néolithique,
VIᵉ millénaire av. l'ère chrétienne, h. 11 cm
Cette figurine, probablement d'une déesse de la fertilité, est particulièrement
remarquable par la position assise, la forme de la tête et du visage,
la couleur rouge qui la recouvre entièrement.

WEIBLICHE TONFIGUR
Chorvat Mincha, Jordantal, Neolithikum, 6. Jahrtausend v. Chr., H. 11 cm
Diese Figur, die möglicherweise eine Fruchtbarkeitsgöttin darstellt,
ist besonders bemerkenswert durch ihre sitzende Stellung, die einmalige Form
des Kopfes und Gesichts und in der die ganze Figur bedeckenden roten Farbe.

צלמית אשה מחרס
חר׳ מנחה, עמק הירדן, תקופת האבן החדשה, האלף הششי לפסה"נ, ג 11 ס"מ

חשיבותה של צלמית זו, המגלמת את דמות אלת הפריון, היא בתנוחת הישיבה המיוחדת,
ובעיצוב הראש והפנים. הצלמית משוחה כולה בצבע אדום.

IVORY STATUETTES OF A MAN AND A WOMAN
Beersheba, Chalcolithic period, 4th millennium BCE, h. 33 and 30 cm

The largest and most remarkable statuettes in the group of "Beersheba ivories",
from the ancient villages lying along the Beersheba riverbed.

STATUETTES D'HOMME ET DE FEMME EN IVOIRE
Beershéba, période chalcolithique, IVe millénaire av. l'ère chrétienne, h. 33 et 30 cm

Ces deux figurines sont les plus grandes, et les plus remarquables aussi,
d'un groupe de statuettes dites «Ivoires de Beershéba» provenant des antiques
villages situés le long de l'oued Beershéba.

ELFENBEIN STATUETTEN EINES MANNES UND EINER FRAU
Beerscheba, Chalkolithikum, 4. Jahrtausend v. Chr., H. 33 und 30 cm

Die größten und bedeutendsten Statuetten der «Beerscheba Elfenbein»-Gruppe,
aus den frühzeitlichen Ansiedlungen entlang dem Beerscheba Flußbett.

צלמיות אשה וגבר משנהב

באר־שבע. התקופה הכלקוליתית. האלף הרביעי לפסה"נ. ג 33 ס"מ. 30 ס"מ

פסלונים אלה הם הגדולים והבולטים ביותר בקבוצת "שנהבי באר־שבע" – צלמיות מן הכפרים
הקדומים שלאורך אפיק נחל באר־שבע.

POTTERY VESSEL IN THE SHAPE OF A WOMAN
Gilat, Western Negev, Chalcolithic period, 4th millennium BCE, h. 30 cm

The vessel, in the form of a nude woman holding a churn on her head, must have
been cultic, connected with fertility and milk.

VASE DE TERRE CUITE EN FORME DE FEMME
Gilat, Négev occidental, période chalcolithique, IVᵉ millénaire av. l'ère chrétienne, h. 30 cm

Ce récipient en forme de femme nue portant une «jatte à lait» sur la tête devait,
probablement, servir dans un culte lié à la fécondité et l'allaitement.

TONGEFÄSS IN FORM EINER FRAU
Gilat, West-Negev, Chalkolithikum, 4. Jahrtausend v. Chr., H. 30 cm

Das Gefäß, das eine nackte Frau, ein Butterfaß auf dem Kopf haltend, darstellt, muß kultische
Bedeutung im Zusammenhang mit Fruchtbarkeit und Milch gehabt haben.

כלי חרס בדמות אשה
גילת, הנגב המערבי, התקופה הכלקוליתית, האלף הרביעי לפסה"נ, ג 30 ס"מ

לכלי זה, בדמות אשה עירומה הנושאת מחבצה על ראשה, היתה בוודאי משמעות פולחנית הקשורה
בחלב ובפוריות.

COPPER MACE HEAD
The Judean Desert Treasure, Chalcolithic period, 4th millennium BCE, h. 11 cm
One of the outstanding objects in the unique treasure of 429 copper and
ivory objects, wrapped in a mat and hidden in the
Cave of the Treasure in Nahal Mishmar.

«TÊTE DE MASSE» EN CUIVRE
Trésor du désert de Judée, période chalcolithique, IVᵉ millénaire
av. l'ère chrétienne, h. 11 cm
L'un des objets remarquables trouvés enveloppés dans une natte dans la
Grotte du Trésor à Nahal Mishmar.
Ce trésor unique comptait 429 objets de cuivre et d'ivoire.

KEULENKOPF AUS KUPFER
Judäischer Wüstenschatz, Chalkolithikum, 4. Jahrtausend v. Chr., H. 11 cm
Eines der hervorragenden Objekte aus dem einzigartigen Fund von 429 Kupfer-
und Elfenbeingegenständen, die in einer Matte gewickelt in der
Schatzhöhle in Nachal Mischmar versteckt lagen.

ראש אֵלה מנחושת
המטמון ממדבר יהודה. התקופה הכלקוליתית. האלף הרביעי לפסה"נ. ג 11 ס"מ

ראש האלה המעוטר הוא בין החפצים הבולטים באוצר של 429 חפצי נחושת ושנהב שנתגלו כשהם
עטופים במחצלת בתוך "מערת מטמון" שבנחל משמר.

POTTERY VESSELS FROM ARAD IN THE NEGEV
Early Canaanite (Bronze) period II, early second millennium BCE, h. 53 and 4.5 cm
The Israel Museum excavations at ancient Arad revealed an extensive and
fortified city, with a wealth of finds in its private and public buildings.

POTERIE D'ARAD DANS LE NÉGEV
Période cananéenne ancienne (Bronze), début du second millénaire
av. l'ère chrétienne, h. 53 et 4,5 cm
Les fouilles entreprises à Arad par le Musée d'Israël ont mis à jour une cité fortifiée;
maints objets ont été trouvés dans les bâtiments publics et privés.

TONGEFÄSSE AUS ARAD IM NEGEV
Frühe kanaanitische (Bronze) Zeit II, frühes 2. Jahrtausend v. Chr., H. 53 und 4,5 cm
Die vom Israel Museum unternommenen Ausgrabungen des alten Arad
brachten eine ausgedehnte befestigte Stadt mit reichen Funden in privaten sowie
öffentlichen Gebäuden zum Vorschein.

כלי חרס מחפירות ערד
התקופה הכנענית (תק' הברונזה) הקדומה, ראשית האלף השלישי לפסה"נ. ג 53; 4.5 ס"מ

חפירות מוזיאון ישראל בערד העתיקה חשפו עיר גדולה ומבוצרת ובה שפע של ממצאים בבתים
הפרטיים ובבנייני הציבור.

POTTERY AND ALABASTER FISH
Tell Poleg, Middle Canaanite (Bronze) IIa period, beginning of second millennium BCE, l. 19 cm
Tell el-Ajjul, Late Canaanite (Bronze) period, 14th-13th century BCE, l. 15 cm

Fish-shaped luxury vessels were popular in the second millennium BCE.

POISSONS DE TERRE CUITE ET D'ALBÂTRE
Tell Poleg, période cananéenne IIa (Bronze), début du second millénaire av. l'ère chrétienne, l. 19 cm
Tell el-Ajjul, période cananéenne récente (Bronze), XIVe-XVe siècle av. l'ère chrétienne, l. 15 cm

Les récipients de luxe façonnés en forme de poisson étaient courants au second
millénaire avant l'ère chrétienne.

KERAMIKFISCH UND ALABASTERFISCH
Tell Poleg, Mittlere kanaanitische (Bronze) IIa Zeit, Anfang des 2. Jahrtausend v. Chr., L. 19 cm
Tell el-Ajjul, Späte kanaanitische (Bronze) Zeit, 14.-13. Jahrhundert v. Chr., L. 15 cm

Prunkgefäße in Fischform kamen im 2. Jahrtausend v. Chr. häufig vor.

דגי חרס ובהט
תל פולג, התקופה הכנענית (תק' הברונזה) התיכונה, ראשית האלף השני לפסה"נ, ג 19 ס"מ
תל אל־עג'ול, התקופה הכנענית (תקופת הברונזה) המאוחרת, המאות הי"ד-הי"ג לפסה"נ, ג 15 ס"מ

באלף השני לפסה"נ מקובל היה לעצב כלים מפוארים בצורת דגים.

GOLD FIGURINES
Gezer, end of Middle Canaanite (Bronze) period,
16th century BCE, h. 10.4 and 16.1 cm
Two figurines of Canaanite goddesses made of sheet gold were found
together with some jewellery, hidden at the city gate.

FIGURINES EN OR
Gézer, fin de la période cananéenne moyenne (Bronze),
XVIe siècle av. l'ère chrétienne, h. 10,4 et 16,1 cm
Deux statuettes de déesses cananéennes en feuille d'or, retrouvées ensemble parmi
d'autres joyaux mis à jour près de la porte de l'antique cité de Gézer.

GOLDFIGURINEN
Gezer, Ende der Mittleren kanaanitischen (Bronze) Zeit,
16. Jahrhundert v. Chr., H. 10,4 und 16,1 cm
Zwei Figurinen aus Blattgold, die kanaanitische Göttinen darstellen, wurden
zusammen mit Schmuck versteckt am Stadttor gefunden.

צלמיות זהב

גזר, סוף התקופה הכנענית (תק' הברונזה) התיכונה, המאה הט"ז לפסה"נ, ג 16.1: 10.4 ס"מ

שתי צלמיות אלו של אלות כנעניות, עשויות מעלה זהב, נתגלו ליד שער העיר, חבויות יחד עם
תכשיטים.

11

POTTERY SARCOPHAGI LIDS
Deir el-Balah, Late Canaanite (Bronze) period,
13th century BCE, h. 65-85 cm

Burial in pottery sarcophagi with sculpted anthropoid lids was common in the
cemetery of Deir el-Balah, in the vicinity of Gaza.

COUVERCLES DE SARCOPHAGES DE TERRE CUITE
Deir el-Balah, période cananéenne récente (Bronze),
XIIIᵉ siècle av. l'ère chrétienne, h. 65-85 cm

De nombreux sarcophages en poterie à couvercles anthropoïdes ont été trouvés dans
le cimetière de Deir el-Balah, non loin de Gaza.

DECKEL VON TONSARKOPHAGEN
Deir el-Balah, Späte kanaanitische (Bronze) Zeit,
13. Jahrhundert v. Chr., H. 65-85 cm

Die Bestattung in Tonsarkophagen mit anthropoid-geformten Deckeln war der
Brauch im Friedhof von Deir el-Balah in der Nähe von Gaza.

מכסים של ארונות־קבורה מחרס

דיר אל־בלח (ליד עזה). התקופה הכנענית (תק' הברונזה) המאוחרת. המאה הי"ג לפסה"נ. ג 65–85 ס"מ

מנהג הקבורה בארונות בעלי מכסים שעליהם מכוירים פני אדם היה רווח בבית־הקברות של
דיר אל־בלח, הקרובה למצרים.

CARNELIAN NECKLACE AND ALABASTER COSMETIC DISH
Deir el-Balah, Late Canaanite (Bronze) period,
13th century BCE, dish h. 8.5 cm

Gold and semi-precious stones, jewellery and cosmetic utensils accompanied
the dead into their graves.

COLLIER DE CORNALINE ET COUPELLE À FARDS D'ALBÂTRE
Deir el-Balah, période cananéenne récente (Bronze),
XIIIᵉ siècle av. l'ère chrétienne, coupelle h. 8,5 cm

Des bijoux, des pierres semi-précieuses, de l'or, des fards accompagnaient les morts
dans leur tombe.

KARNEOL-HALSKETTE UND ALABASTER-KOSMETIKSCHALE
Deir el-Balah, Späte kanaanitische (Bronze) Zeit,
13. Jahrhundert v. Chr., Schale H. 8,5 cm

Gold, Halbedelsteine, Schmuck und Kosmetik-Utensilien wurden den
Toten mit ins Grab gegeben.

מחרוזת קרניאול וקערית תמרוקים מבהט
דיר אל-בלח, התקופה הכנענית (תק' הברונזה) המאוחרת, המאה הי"ג לפסה"נ
ג הקערית: 8.5 ס"מ

תכשיטים רבים של זהב ואבנים טובות-למחצה וכלי תמרוקים של בהט הונחו עם המתים בקבריהם.

13

II

THE ISRAELITES AND THEIR NEIGHBOURS

Consolidation of the Israelites as a national and political entity under the monarchy,
alongside the Canaanites, the sea-faring peoples and the trans-Jordan kingdoms.
Integration of local and peripheral stylistic elements in art and decoration,
ranging from everyday vessels to royal edifices.
Hebrew script, written in ink or incised on seals and pottery vessels,
reflecting the diffusion of literacy.

LES ISRAÉLITES ET LEURS VOISINS

Raffermissement de l'entité nationale et politique des Israélites sous la monarchie.
Leurs voisins sont les Cananéens, les Peuples de la mer et les Royaumes d'outre-Jourdain.
Intégration d'éléments stylistiques locaux et périphériques dans l'art et la décoration,
depuis les objets quotidiens jusqu'au Palais de Samarie.
L'écriture hébraïque, tracée à l'encre ou gravée sur des sceaux et des poteries,
reflète la diffusion de l'écriture et de la lecture.

DIE ISRAELITEN UND IHRE NACHBARN

Die Konsolidierung der Israeliten zu einer nationalen und politischen
Einheit unter der Monarchie, neben den Kanaanitern, den Seevölkern und den
transjordanischen Königreichen.
Die Integrierung lokaler und peripherer Stilelemente in Kunst und Dekoration
vom täglichen Gebrauchsobjekt bis zum Palast von Samaria.
Die hebräische Schrift, eingeritzt in Siegel und Tongefässe oder mit Tinte geschrieben,
Zeugnis für die Verbreitung des Lesens und Schreibens.

הישראלים ושכניהם

התגבשות בני-ישראל לאומה, לישות פוליטית ולממלכה, לצד הכנענים, גויי-הים והממלכות
שבעבר-הירדן. התמזגות יסודות סגנוניים מקומיים ופריפריים באמנות ובעיטור – מכלי יום-יום לפריטים מארמון
המלכות בשומרון. הכתב העברי, כתוב בדיו או חרות על-גבי חותמות
וכלי-חרס, כמשקף את תפוצת ידע הקרוא-וכתוב.

DECORATED POTTERY BOWL AND JUG
Ashkelon and Ashdod, Early Israelite (Iron) period,
12th century BCE, h. 11.5 and 26 cm

The jug, presumably used for storing beer, and the bowl, are outstanding
examples of the style of painted decoration attributed to the
Philistines in the early Iron Age.

COUPE ET CRUCHE DÉCORÉES EN TERRE CUITE
Ashkelon et Ashdod, période israélienne ancienne (Fer),
XIIe siècle av. l'ère chrétienne, h. 11,5 et 26 cm

La cruche, servant à la bière sans doute, et la coupe, sont des exemplaires
remarquables de la décoration peinte attribuée aux Philistins à l'âge de Fer ancien.

VERZIERTE SCHALE UND KRUG AUS TON
Aschkalon und Aschdod, Frühe Israelische (Eisen) Zeit,
12. Jahrhundert v. Chr., H. 11,5 und 26 cm

Der Krug, vermutlich ein Biergefäß, und die Schale sind hervorragende Beispiele
des dekorativen Stils der Philister in der frühen Eisenzeit.

פך וקערית מעוטרים מחרס

אשדוד ואשקלון, התקופה הישראלית (תק' הברזל) הקדומה, המאה הי"ב לפסה"נ, ג. 26: 11.5 ס"מ

הפכית, ששימשה כנראה לאחסנת בירה, וכן הספל הם שניהם דוגמאות מעולות לסגנון העיטור המיוחס
לפלשתים בתקופה זו.

BRONZE BULL STATUETTE
Samaria, Early Israelite (Iron) period, 12th century BCE, h. 12.5 cm
This statuette may be related to the cult of Hadad, the West-Semitic storm god, one of whose attributes was the bull.

STATUETTE DE TAUREAU EN BRONZE
Samarie, période israélite ancienne (Fer), XIIᵉ siècle av. l'ère chrétienne, h. 12,5 cm
Cette sculpture est probablement liée au culte de Hadad le dieu de l'Orage des peuples sémites de l'Ouest, dont un des attributs était le taureau.

BRONZE-STATUETTE EINES STIERS
Samaria, Frühe Israelitische (Eisen) Zeit, 12. Jahrhundert v. Chr., H. 12,5 cm
Diese Statuette ist wahrscheinlich dem Kult des Hadad zuzuschreiben. Hadad war der westsemitische Sturmgott. Der Stier war eines seiner Tierattribute.

צלמית שור מברונזה

שומרון, התקופה הישראלית (תק' הברזל) הקדומה, המאה הי"ב לפסה"נ ג 12.5 ס"מ

צלמית זו קשורה אולי לפולחן הדד, אל הסערה השמי-מערבי, אשר השור היה בעל-החיים המשויך אליו.

POTTERY CULT-STAND TOPPED WITH BOWL
Ashdod, Early Israelite (Iron) period, 10th century BCE, h. 35 cm
The role of musicians in cult ceremonies is reflected here in the five
figures, playing different instruments, incorporated into
the walls of the stand.

SUPPORT RITUEL SURMONTÉ D'UNE COUPE EN TERRE CUITE
Ashdod, période israélite ancienne (Fer) Xᵉ siècle av. l'ère chrétienne, h. 35 cm
Le rôle de la musique dans les cérémonies religieuses
est attesté ici par les motifs choisis: cinq musiciens jouant d'instruments
différents incorporés dans le socle.

KULT-STÄNDER MIT SCHALE AUS TON
Aschdod, Frühe Israelitische (Eisen) Zeit, 10. Jahrhundert v. Chr., H. 35 cm
Die Rolle von Musikanten im kultischen Zeremoniell spiegelt sich hier in
den fünf Figuren wider, die verschiedene Instrumente spielend,
in die Wände des Ständers eingegliedert sind.

כן פולחני ועליו קערית מחרס
אשדוד. התקופה הישראלית (תק' הברזל) הקדומה, המאה הי' לפסה"נ. ג 35 ס"מ

חמש דמויות הנגנים המעוצבות בחללים שבדפנות הכן. המנגנות בכלים שונים. מצביעות על מקומה של
הנגינה בטקסי הפולחן.

IVORY WINGED SPHINX
Samaria, Israelite (Iron) period, 9th-8th century BCE, h. 7.5 cm
Open-work Phoenician ivory plaque, probably used as
inlay in wooden furniture.

SPHINX AILÉ EN IVOIRE
Samarie, période israélite (Fer), IXᵉ-VIIIᵉ siècle av. l'ère chrétienne, h. 7,5 cm
Plaque d'ivoire phénicienne sculptée à jour qui a dû servir
d'ornement incrusté dans un meuble de bois.

GEFLÜGELTE SPHINX AUS ELFENBEIN
Samaria, Israelitische (Eisen) Zeit, 9.-8. Jahrhundert v. Chr., H. 7,5 cm
Durchbrochenes phönizisches Elfenbeinplättchen, vermutlich
als Einlage für Holzmöbel benutzt.

ספינקס מכונף משנהב
שומרון, התקופה הישראלית (תק' הברזל), המאוחרת, המאה הט'-הח' לפסה"נ, ג 7.5 ס"מ

לוחית שנהב עשויה מעשה-סבכה, אשר שובצה בוודאי כעיטור ברהיטי עץ.

STONE HEAD OF A BEARDED MALE
Ammonite style, Iron Age, 9th-7th century BCE, h. 43.8 cm

The head, with its high Egyptian-style headdress, diadem and earrings,
recalls royal figures from Mesopotamia and Syria, indicating that
it too might have represented a ruler.

TÊTE D'HOMME À BARBE EN PIERRE
Style ammonite, âge du Fer, IXᵉ-VIIᵉ siècle av. l'ère chrétienne, h. 43,8 cm

La haute coiffure de style égyptien, le diadème et les boucles d'oreilles
rappellent les images royales de Mésopotamie et de Syrie, ce qui laisse à penser
qu'il pourrait bien s'agir d'une tête de souverain.

HAUPT EINES BÄRTIGEN MANNES, STEIN
Ammonitischer Stil, Eisenzeit, 9.-7. Jahrhundert v. Chr., H. 43,8 cm

Der Kopf erinnert mit seinem hohen Kopfputz in ägyptischem Stil,
dem Diadem und den Ohrringen an königliche Figuren aus Mesopotamien und Syrien,
woraus man schließen kann, daß es sich vielleicht auch hier um einen Herrscher handelt.

ראש גבר מזוקן מאבן
סגנון עמוני, התקופה הישראלית (תק' הברזל) המאוחרת, המאות הט'-הז' לפסה"נ, ג 43.8 ס"מ

הראש, על תסרוקתו הגבוהה בסגנון מצרי, הנזר והעגילים, מזכיר דמויות מלכותיות ממסופוטמיה
ומסוריה ומעלה בכך את האפשרות שהוא מייצג דמות שליט.

POTTERY JUG
Jerusalem, City of David, late 8th century BCE, h. 20 cm

This fine specimen of First Temple pottery was incised after firing with the name
of its owner: "(Belongs) to Eliyahu".

POT DE TERRE
Jérusalem, Cité de David, fin du VIIIᵉ siècle av. l'ère chrétienne, h. 20 cm

Très beau spécimen de poterie de l'époque du Premier Temple
gravé après cuisson au nom de son propriétaire:
«(Appartient) à Eliahou».

TONKRUG
Jerusalem, David-Stadt, Spätes 8. Jahrhundert v. Chr., H. 20 cm

Ein schönes Exemplar der Keramik aus der Zeit des Ersten Tempels. Der Name
des Besitzers, «(Gehört) dem Eliahu», wurde erst nach
dem Brennprozeß eingeritzt.

פך חרס
ירושלים, עיר דוד, סוף המאה הח' לפסה"נ, ג 20 ס"מ

כלי זה, שעליו נחרת השם "לאליהו" לאחר הצריפה, מצטיין בעיצובו הנאה ומאפיין את כלי החרס
מתקופת הבית הראשון.

HEBREW SEALS
Israelite (Iron) period II, 8th-6th century BCE, h. 0.7-1.8 cm

Scaraboid seals, mostly of semi-precious stones or hard limestone, incised in
the ancient Hebrew script, bearing the names of their owners. The seal-impression
was used as a mark of ownership, to authenticate documents.

SCEAUX HÉBRAÏQUES
Période israélite II (Fer), VIIIᵉ-VIᵉ siècle av. l'ère chrétienne, h. 0,7-1,8 cm

Sceaux dits «scarabées» en pierres semi-précieuses ou calcaire
dur pour la plupart, aux noms de leurs propriétaires gravés en caractères hébraïques
de type ancien. L'empreinte des sceaux était employée pour marquer
et authentifier des documents.

HEBRÄISCHE SIEGEL
Israelitische (Eisen) Zeit II, 8.-6. Jahrhundert v. Chr., H. 0,7-1,8 cm

Scarabaeoide Siegel, meistens aus Halbedelsteinen oder hartem Kreidestein,
mit dem Namen des Besitzers, in althebräischer Schrift, eingraviert.
Siegeldrucke bestätigten den Eigentümer und wurden zur Beglaubigung
der Dokumente benutzt.

חותמות עבריים

התקופה הישראלית (תק' הברזל) המאוחרת, המאות הח'-הו' לפסה"נ, ג' 0.7-1.8 ס"מ

חותמות דמויי חרפושית. רובם מאבנים טובות-למחצה או מאבן-גיר קשה, חקוקים בכתב העברי הקדום
ונושאים את שם בעליהם. טביעת החותם שימשה כאישור וסימן לבעלות, כפי שמשמשת היום
חתימת ידו של אדם.

POTTERY VESSELS
En Gedi, late Judaean Kingdom, early 6th century BCE, h. 10-20 cm

These vessels were uncovered in a site consisting mainly of workshops and
installations that were probably used for the production of perfume.

VASES DE POTERIE
En Gedi, Monarchie de Judée, début du VIᵉ siècle av. l'ère chrétienne, h. 10-20 cm

Ces poteries ont été découvertes dans un lieu où se trouvaient
essentiellement des vestiges d'ateliers et d'installations destinées probablement
à la production de parfums.

KERAMIKGEFÄSSE
En Gedi, spätes Jüdisches Königreich, frühes 6. Jahrhundert v. Chr., H. 10-20 cm

Diese Gefäße wurden an einem Ort freigelegt, wo sich hauptsächlich Werkstätten und
Anlagen befanden, die wahrscheinlich zur Parfümherstellung dienten.

כלי חרס

עין־גדי, סוף ימי ממלכת יהודה, ראשית המאה הו' לפסה"נ, ג 10־20 ס"מ

כלים אלה התגלו ביישוב שהכיל בעיקר בתי־מלאכה ומתקנים, כנראה לייצור בושם.

21

THREE GLASS AMPHORISKOI
Eastern Mediterranean, 6th-5th century BCE, h. 7.1-7.2 cm
Small colourful vessels, imitating the shape of large Greek pottery amphorae,
shaped on a core in the technique of glass-making prevalent
before glass-blowing was invented.

TROIS AMPHORES DE VERRE
Méditerranée orientale, VIe-Ve siècle av. l'ère chrétienne, h. 7,1-7,2 cm
Ces petites amphores hautes en couleur,
imitant les grandes amphores de poterie grecques, étaient façonnées autour d'un «noyau»
selon la technique employée avant la découverte du verre soufflé.

DREI GLASAMPHORISKOI
Östlicher Mittelmeerraum, 6.-5. Jahrhundert v. Chr., H. 7,1-7,2 cm
Diese kleinen farbfreudigen Gefäße, die die Form großer griechischer Tonamphorae
nachahmen, wurden auf einem Kern geformt.
Diese Technik der Glasherstellung ging der Erfindung der Glasbläserei voraus.

3 קנקניות מזכוכית
מזרח הים התיכון, המאות הו'-הה' לפסה"נ, ג. 7.2-7.1 ס"מ

כלים צבעוניים קטנים אלה, המחקים בצורתם אמפורות חרס יווניות גדולות, נוצרו בשיטת הליבה,
שהיתה רווחת עד שהומצאה שיטת ניפוח הזכוכית.

22

THE TEL ZIPPOR HOARD
Tel Zippor, Hellenistic period, c. 300 BCE, juglet h. 15 cm

The pottery vessel, pierced to be used as a cash box, contained
fifty-nine silver tetradrachms of Alexander the Great and his diadochs,
together with three locally struck silver Athenian drachms.

LE TRÉSOR DE TEL ZIPPOR
Tel Zippor, période hellénistique, env. 300 av. l'ère chrétienne, cruchon h. 15 cm

Cette poterie, trouée pour servir de «tirelire»,
contenait 59 tétradrachmes d'argent d'Alexandre le Grand et ses diadoques
et trois drachmes athéniens en argent frappés dans la région.

DER TEL-ZIPPOR-SCHATZ
Tel Zippor, Hellenistische Zeit, um 300 v. Chr., Krug H. 15 cm

Das Keramikgefäß, in das ein Loch gebrochen wurde, um als Behälter
für Münzen zu dienen, enthielt 59 Silbertetradrachmen aus der Zeit Alexanders
des Großen und seiner Diadochen und drei lokal gemünzte Athenische Silberdrachmen.

מטמון תל ציפור
תל ציפור, התקופה ההלניסטית, 300 לפסה"נ בקירוב, ג' הפבית: 15 ס"מ

כד חרס שנוקב בו חור כדי שישמש קופה ובו 59 סלעי כסף מימי אלכסנדר מוקדון ויורשיו וכן שלוש
דרכמות כסף אתונאיות שנטבעו בארץ.

23

III

JEWISH, ROMAN, CHRISTIAN AND ISLAMIC PALESTINE

The heyday of Jewish Palestine under the Herodian dynasty.
Loss of independence, leading to increased dependency of the province on changing centres –
Rome, Byzantium, Damascus, Baghdad and Cairo.
Expansion of the concept of Palestine as the Holy Land with the growth of Christianity.
Apogee of architecture, mosaic and glass production.

LA PALESTINE JUIVE, ROMAINE, CHRÉTIENNE ET ISLAMIQUE

Les beaux jours de la Palestine juive sous la dynastie hérodienne.
Après la perte de l'indépendance, le pays devient une province dépendant de centres se situant
tour à tour à Rome, Byzance, Damas, Baghdad et le Caire.
Le concept de la Terre Promise s'étend avec la croissance du christianisme.
Apogée de l'architecture, de la mosaïque et du verre.

JÜDISCHES, RÖMISCHES, CHRISTLICHES UND ISLAMISCHES PALÄSTINA

Blütezeit des jüdischen Palästinas unter der Herodianischen Dynastie.
Das Land nach dem Verlust seiner Unabhängigkeit – eine von wechselnden Mächten abhängige
Provinz, unter denen Rom, Byzanz, Damaskus, Bagdad und Kairo zu den wichtigsten zählen.
Entwicklung des Begriffes Palästina als heiliges Land mit
der Verbreitung des Christentums.
Höhepunkt der Baukunst, der Mosaik- und Glasproduktion.

ארץ־ישראל – צומת של יהדות, הלניות, נצרות ואסלאם
פריחתה של ארץ ישראל היהודית בימי הורדוס וביתו. אבדן העצמאות.
יהודה פרובינקיה בשלטון ממלכות מתחלפות: רומא, ביזנטיון, דמשק, בגדאד וקאהיר. התרחבות מושג
"ארץ־הקודש" עם התפשטות הנצרות. תקופות שיא באדריכלות, בפסיפס ובייצור זכוכית.

GRAFFITO OF THE MENORAH
Jerusalem, Second Temple period,
first century CE - 70 CE, h. 20 cm

Originally from a wall of a house in the Upper City
of Jerusalem, this depiction was contemporary with the Temple Menorah
and is an eye-witness representation of it.

GRAFFITO DE LA MENORAH
Jérusalem, période du Second Temple,
Ier siècle de l'ère chrétienne - 70 de l'ère chrétienne, h. 20 cm

Ce graffito était gravé à l'origine sur le mur d'une
maison de la ville haute de Jérusalem. Cela doit être l'œuvre d'un témoin qui
lui-même avait vu la menorah au Temple.

GRAFFITO DER MENORAH
Jerusalem, Zeit des Zweiten Tempels,
1. Jahrhundert n. Chr. - 70 n. Chr., H. 20 cm

Diese Darstellung, die ursprünglich in die Wand eines Hauses der Oberstadt
Jerusalem eingeritzt war, mag von einem Augenzeugen stammen,
der die Tempel-Menorah kannte.

מנורת שבעת הקנים חרותה על טיח
ירושלים, תקופת הבית השני, המאה הא' לסה"נ-70 לסה"נ, ג. 20 ס"מ

תיאור זה של המנורה, שהיה במקורו על קיר בית בעיר העליונה בירושלים, הוא בן זמנה של מנורת
המקדש ונעשה בוודאי בידי מי שראה אותה בעיניו.

ISAIAH SCROLL, MS.A
Qumran, c. 100 BCE

Four of the fifty-four columns of the parchment scroll
(total length 7.34 m). Fragments of almost all the Old Testament books were
discovered in Qumran, but this is the only one found in its entirety.

LE ROULEAU D'ISAÏE, MS.A
Qumran, env. 100 av. l'ère chrétienne

Quatre colonnes de ce rouleau de parchemin qui en comprend
cinquante-quatre (d'une longueur totale de 7,34 m).
Des fragments de presque tous les livres de la Bible ont été découverts
à Qumran; seul, le Rouleau d'Isaïe est entier.

JESAJA-ROLLE, MS.A
Qumran, um 100 v. Chr.

Vier der vierundfünfzig Kolumnen
der Pergamentrolle (Gesamtlänge 7,34 m). In Qumran wurden
Fragmente von fast allen Büchern des Alten
Testamentes entdeckt, diese Rolle ist jedoch die einzige,
die einen vollständigen Text enthält.

מגילת ישעיהו, כת״י א׳
קומראן, 100 לפסה״נ בקירוב

ארבעה מתוך חמישים וארבעה הטורים של מגילת הקלף (אורכה הכולל 7.34 מ׳). בקומראן נתגלו כמעט
כל ספרי המקרא, אבל זהו הספר היחיד שנמצא בשלמותו.

FINDS FROM THE JEWISH QUARTER EXCAVATIONS
IN THE OLD CITY OF JERUSALEM
Second Temple period, first century CE

Mosaics, stone vessels and furnishings of soft limestone,
typical of the patrician life-style of Jerusalem's Upper City on the eve of its
destruction by the Romans in 70 CE.

OBJETS MIS À JOUR LORS DE FOUILLES DANS LA
VIEILLE VILLE DE JÉRUSALEM
Période du Second Temple, Ier siècle de l'ère chrétienne

Mosaïques, ustensiles et meubles de
pierre témoignent de la vie luxueuse des résidents de la Ville Haute à la
veille de la destruction de Jérusalem en 70.

FUNDE AUS DEN AUSGRABUNGEN IM JÜDISCHEN VIERTEL
DER ALTSTADT JERUSALEM
Zeit des Zweiten Tempels, 1. Jahrhundert n. Chr.

Mosaiken, Steingefäße und Mobiliar aus weichem Kalkstein, typisch
für den Lebensstil der Patrizier der Jerusalemer Oberstadt, am Vorabend ihrer
Zerstörung durch die Römer im Jahre 70 n. Chr.

ממצאים מן החפירות ברובע היהודי בירושלים
תקופת הבית השני, המאה הא' לסה"נ

קטעי פסיפס, כלים ורהיטים מאבן־גיר רכה האופייניים לסגנון החיים של בני המעמד הגבוה בעיר
העליונה של ירושלים ערב החורבן, בשנת 70 לסה"נ.

VESSELS FROM THE PERIOD OF THE BAR KOKHBA REVOLT
Cave of Letters, Judaean Desert,
c. 135 CE, jug h. 19 cm

In the aftermath of the revolt, residents of the
En Gedi oasis found temporary shelter in this cave. Its unusual climatic
conditions helped preserve an extensive assemblage of
objects, including vessels made of organic materials, rare finds in
Palestinian archaeology.

RÉCIPIENTS DE L'ÉPOQUE DE LA RÉVOLTE DE BAR KOCHBA
Grotte des Lettres, Désert de Judée,
env. 135 de l'ère chrétienne, cruche h. 19 cm

Après la révolte, des habitants de l'oasis d'En Gedi
cherchèrent refuge dans cette grotte. Parmi un groupe important d'objets
parfaitement conservés grâce aux conditions climatiques,
on a trouvé des récipients en matières organiques –
très rares dans l'archéologie palestinienne.

GEFÄSSE AUS DER ZEIT DES BAR-KOCHBA-AUFSTANDES
Höhle der Briefe, Judäaische Wüste,
um 135 n. Chr., Krug H. 19 cm

Nach dem Aufstand fanden die Bewohner der En-Gedi-Oasis
in dieser Höhle Zuflucht. Durch die ungewöhnlichen klimatischen
Bedingungen dieser Umgebung blieben eine große Zahl von
Gegenständen erhalten, darunter auch solche aus organischen
Materialien, seltene Funde in der palästinensischen Archäologie.

חפצים מימי מרד בר־כוכבא
מערת האגרות, מדבר יהודה, 135 לסה"נ בקירוב, ג הפך: 19 ס"מ

בשלהי המרד מצאו מקלט במערה זו כמה מתושבי עין־גדי. תנאי האקלים של המערה שימרו אוסף גדול
של חפצים של אותם מורדים ובתוכם גם כלים העשויים חומרים אורגניים. ממצאים נדירים
בארכיאולוגיה של ארץ־ישראל.

IRON PARADE HELMET
Roman, 2nd century CE, h. 26 cm

Helmets such as this were worn by the auxiliary
forces in the provinces of the empire during parades and special events.

CASQUE DE PARADE EN FER
Période romaine, IIᵉ siècle de l'ère chrétienne, h. 26 cm

Les forces auxiliaires dans les provinces de l'Empire romain portaient de
tels casques lors de parades ou d'événements importants.

EISENER PARADEHELM
Römisch, 2. Jahrhundert n. Chr., H. 26 cm

Solche Helme wurden von den Hilfstruppen in den Reichsprovinzen
während Paraden und zu besonderen Anlässen getragen.

קסדת מצעדים מברזל
רומאית, המאה הב' לסה"נ, ג 26 ס"מ

קסדות מעין זו חבשו חילות־העזר בפרובינקיות של האימפריה בעת מצעדים ובאירועים מיוחדים.

THE EMPEROR HADRIAN (117-138)
Tel Shalem, h. 82 cm

Bronze statue of the Emperor which was found on the site of a camp of the
6th Roman Legion, near Beth Shean. While numerous
marble statues representing Hadrian have survived, this excellent portrait is one of the
two cuirassed bronze statues of the Emperor known to date.

L'EMPEREUR HADRIEN (117-138)
Tel Shalem, h. 82 cm

Statue de bronze trouvée dans le site du camp de la 6e Légion romaine, près
de Beth Shéan. Tandis que de nombreux portraits en marbre d'Hadrien ont survécu,
cet excellent portrait est une des deux statues en bronze
représentant l'empereur en cuirasse que nous connaissions à ce jour.

KAISER HADRIAN (117-138)
Tel Schalem, H. 82 cm

Die Bronzestatue wurde in der Nähe von Beth Schean gefunden, am
Ort wo einst die 6. Römische Legion ein Lager hatte. Während man zahlreiche
Marmor Statuen Hadrians kennt, ist dieses hervorragende Porträt eines der
zwei bis jetzt bekannten Bronze Statuen, die den Kaiser in Panzerrüstung darstellen.

הדריאנוס קיסר (117-138 לסה"נ)
תל שלם, ג 82 ס"מ

פסל ברונזה של הקיסר, שנמצא באתר מחנה הלגיון הרומאי הששי ליד בית־שאן. מצויים כיום בידינו
פסלי שיש רבים ביותר של הדריאנוס. אך דיוקן מעולה זה, שעד כה נמצא רק עוד אחד כמותו, מתייחד
בכך שהוא עשוי ברונזה ומתאר את הקיסר עוטה שריון.

JEWELLERY OF THE LATE ROMAN PERIOD
Kefar Giladi and Jerusalem, 3rd century CE,
l. 28.3 cm, h. 5.3 cm

Gold diadem set with coloured stones from a
mausoleum at Kefar Giladi, and gold brooch set with an onyx depicting
Athena, found in Jerusalem.

BIJOUX DE LA FIN DE LA PÉRIODE ROMAINE
Kefar Giladi et Jérusalem, IIIᵉ siècle de l'ère chrétienne,
l. 28,3 cm, h. 5,3 cm

Diadème d'or incrusté de pierres de
couleurs, trouvé dans un mausolée à Kefar Giladi; broche en or sertie
d'une image d'Athéna en onyx, mise à jour à Jérusalem.

SCHMUCK AUS SPÄTRÖMISCHER ZEIT
Kefar Giladi und Jerusalem, 3. Jahrhundert n. Chr.,
L. 28,3 cm, H. 5,3 cm

Golddiadem mit Farbsteinen, aus
einem Mausoleum in Kefar Giladi; Goldbrosche aus Jerusalem
mit einem Onyx Athena darstellend, besetzt.

תכשיטים מן התקופה הרומית המאוחרת
כפר-גלעדי וירושלים, המאה הג' לסה"נ, ר הנזר: 28.3 ס"מ: ג הסיכה 5.3 ס"מ

נזר זהב משובץ באבנים צבעוניות, נמצא במאוזוליאום בכפר-גלעדי, וכן סיכת זהב משובצת באוניקס
שעליו חרותה דמות אתנה, נמצאה בירושלים.

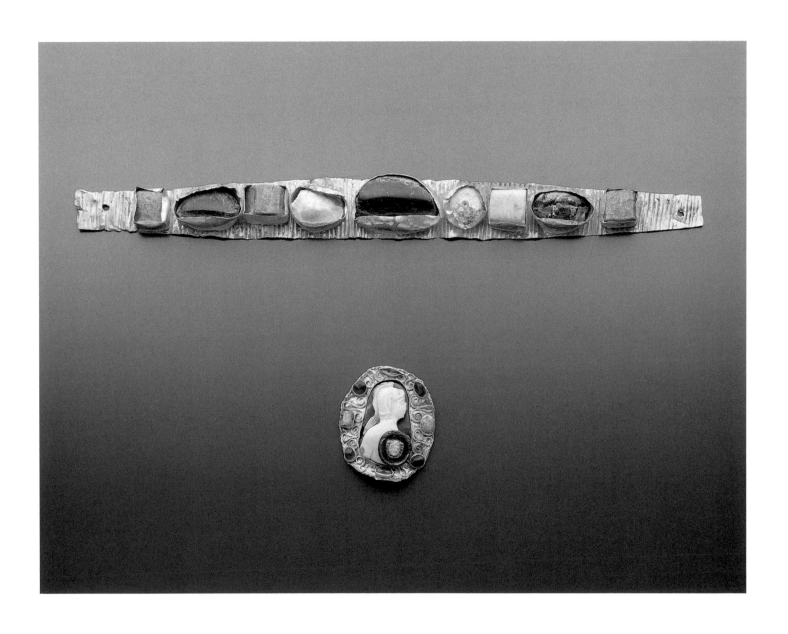

SEGMENT OF A MOSAIC FLOOR
Shechem (Neapolis), Late Roman period,
3rd century CE, h. 128 cm

From a mosaic floor of a Roman villa triclinium.
The picture shows a segment of the mosaic's border which is decorated with
depictions of human faces, animals and hunting scenes.

FRAGMENT DE PAVEMENT DE MOSAÏQUE
Shechem (Neapolis), période romaine,
IIIᵉ siècle de l'ère chrétienne, h. 128 cm

Fragment d'un pavement de mosaïque du triclinium d'une villa romaine.
L'illustration choisie représente une partie de la
bordure ornée de faces humaines, d'animaux et de scènes de chasse.

TEIL EINES MOSAIKBODENS
Sichem (Neapolis), Spätrömische Zeit,
3. Jahrhundert n. Chr., H. 128 cm

Vom Mosaikboden des Trikliniums einer römischen Villa.
Das Bild zeigt ein Detail der Mosaikumrandung die Darstellungen von
menschlichen Gesichtern, Tieren und Jagdszenen enthält.

קטע מרצפת פסיפס
שכם. התקופה הרומית המאוחרת. המאה הג' לסה"נ. א 128 ס"מ

פסיפס של רצפת טרקלין מווילה רומאית. בתצלום קטע מן המסגרת המעוטרת בפני אדם, דמויות חיות
ותמונות ציד.

GIANT GLASS JUG
Eretz Israel-Syria (Byzantine period),
4th-5th century CE, h. 31.3 cm

One of a group of elaborate jugs of the early Byzantine
period decorated in various techniques and constituting a pinnacle
of glass-making of all periods.

PICHET DE VERRE GÉANT
Eretz-Israël-Syrie, époque byzantine,
IV-Ve siècle, h. 31,3 cm

Cette pièce fait partie d'un groupe de vases d'une très
belle facture, datant du début de la période byzantine. Ils sont exécutés dans
diverses techniques et comptent parmi les
chefs-d'œuvre de l'art de la verrerie de tous les temps.

RIESENKRUG AUS GLAS
Eretz Israel-Syrien, byzantinische Zeit,
4.-5. Jahrhundert n. Chr., H. 31,3 cm

Dieses außergewöhnliche Gefäß gehört zu einer Gruppe von
kunstvollen Krügen aus der frühen byzantinischen Zeit, die in verschiedenen
Techniken dekoriert sind und einen der
Höhepunkte der Glaskunst aller Zeiten bilden.

פך ענק מזכוכית
א״י-סוריה, התקופה הביזנטית, המאות הד׳-הה׳ לסה״נ ג 31.3 ס״מ

כלי יחיד במינו זה, שאין לו מקבילות, משתייך לקבוצה של פכים מפוארים מן התקופה הביזנטית. הפכים
עוטרו בטכניקות שונות והם מהווים אחד משיאי אמנות הזכוכית בכל התקופות.

BRONZE OIL LAMP
Byzantine period, h. 11.5 cm

A large oil lamp typical of the period, bearing a cross
on the handle.

LAMPE À HUILE EN BRONZE
Epoque byzantine, h. 11,5 cm

Lampe à huile typique de cette époque, d'assez grande
dimension et ornée d'une croix sur la poignée.

ÖL-LAMPE AUS BRONZE
Byzantinische Zeit, H. 11,5 cm

Eine große Öl-Lampe, typisch für diese Zeit, mit einem
Kreuz auf dem Griff.

נר שמן מברונזה
התקופה הביזנטית. ג 11.5 ס"מ

נר שמן אופייני לתקופה ולו ידית גבוהה מעוטרת בצלב.

BRONZE MENORAH
En Gedi, Talmudic period, 6th century CE, h. 14 cm

The menorah was found in the excavation of the
ancient synagogue of En Gedi, a flourishing Jewish settlement during
the Roman and Byzantine periods.

CHANDELIER À SEPT BRANCHES DE BRONZE
En Gedi, période talmudique, VIe siècle, h. 14 cm

Cette menorah a été découverte lors de
fouilles dans l'antique synagogue d'En Gedi qui était une ville
juive florissante aux périodes romaine et byzantine.

MENORAH AUS BRONZE
En Gedi, Talmudische Zeit, 6. Jahrhundert n. Chr., H. 14 cm

Die Menorah wurde während der Ausgrabung der
antiken Synagoge in En Gedi, einer blühenden jüdischen Siedlung in
römischer und byzantinischen Zeit, gefunden.

מנורת שבעת הקנים מברונזה
עין־גדי. תקופת התלמוד. המאה הו' לסה"נ. ג 14 ס"מ

המנורה נמצאה בחפירות בית־הכנסת הקדום בעין־גדי. שהיה יישוב יהודי משגשג בתקופה הרומית
והביזנטית.

POTTERY PILGRIM FLASKS
Byzantine period, 6th century CE, h. 8-14 cm

Ampullae with Christian holy scenes that were filled with water from
the Jordan and cherished by pilgrims to the Holy Land.

«GOURDES DE PÈLERINS» EN TERRE CUITE
Epoque byzantine, XIᵉ siècle, h. 8-14 cm

Flasques sphériques ornées de thèmes sacrés qui étaient
remplies d'eau du Jourdain. Elles étaient fort prisées des pèlerins chrétiens
en Terre Sainte.

PILGERFLASCHEN AUS TON
Byzantinische Zeit, 6. Jahrhundert n. Chr., H. 8-14 cm

Kleine Gefässe mit Darstellungen von
christlichen Szenen. Mit Jordanwasser gefüllt, waren sie beliebt bei Pilgern
die das Heilige Land besuchten.

צפחות צליינים מחרס

התקופה הביזנטית. המאה הו' לסה"נ. ג' 8-14 ס"מ

צליינים נוהגים היו לקחת עמם מארץ־הקודש צפחות מעוטרות בתמונות נוצריות ומלאות במי הירדן.

MOSAIC FLOOR
El-Makr (Western Galilee), Byzantine period,
5th century CE, h. 350 cm

Probably originating from a church or monastery, this floor demonstrates
the best of the geometric style of the period.

MOSAÏQUE DE SOL
El-Makr (Galilée occidentale), époque byzantine,
Ve siècle, h. 350 cm

Provenant vraisemblablement d'une église
ou d'un monastère, ce pavement atteste la haute qualité de la décoration
géométrique de l'époque.

BODENMOSAIK
El-Makr (Westgaliläa), Byzantinische Zeit,
5. Jahrhundert n. Chr., H. 350 cm

Dieses Bodenmosaik, das wahrscheinlich von einer
Kirche oder einem Kloster stammt, ist eines der besten Beispiele des
geometrischen Stils dieser Epoche.

רצפת פסיפס

אל־מכר, הגליל המערבי, התקופה הביזנטית, המאה הה' לסה"נ, א 350 ס"מ

הפסיפס, שמקורו כנראה בכנסייה או במנזר, עשוי במיטב הסגנון הגיאומטרי של התקופה.

JEWELLERY HOARD
Caesarea, Fatimid period, 11th century CE,
vase, h. 11 cm

The gold beads are made of sheet-gold or wire
worked in the filigree technique. The silver items are decorated
in niello with Arabic calligraphy.

TRÉSOR DE BIJOUX
Césarée, époque fatimide, XIᵉ siècle,
vase, h. 11 cm

Les perles sont faites de feuille ou de fils d'or travaillés en filigrane.
Les pièces d'argent sont ornées de calligraphie arabe niellée.

SCHMUCKSCHATZ
Caesarea, Fatimidische Zeit, 11. Jahrhundert n. Chr.,
Vase, H. 11 cm

Die Goldperlen bestehen aus Goldblatt oder Golddraht
in Filigrantechnik verarbeitet. Die Silberanhänger sind mit arabischen
Schriftzeichen in Niello dekoriert.

אוצר תכשיטים
קיסריה, התקופה הפאטימית, המאה הי"א לסה"נ, ג הכד: 11 ס"מ

חרוזי הזהב עשויים מעלי זהב או בטכניקת פיליגראן ותכשיטי הכסף מעוטרים בכתב בטכניקת ניאלו.

LEAD BULLA
Jerusalem, Crusader period,
12th century CE, diam. 4.5 cm

Seal-impression of Amalricus de Nesle, the Ninth Latin
Patriarch of Jerusalem. Obverse: a five-line
Latin inscription, "Amalricus Sanctae Resurrectionis Ecclesiae Patriarcha";
reverse: a representation of the
Resurrection conceived as the descent of Christ in limbo.

BULLE DE PLOMB
Jérusalem, époque des Croisades,
XIIᵉ siècle, diam. 4,5 cm

Sceau d'Amalric de Nesle, Neuvième Patriarche
latin de Jérusalem. Sur l'avers, une inscription en latin: «Amalricus
Sanctae Resurrectionis Ecclesiae
Patriarcha»; sur le revers, une image de la Résurrection conçue
comme la descente du Christ dans les limbes.

BLEI-BULLE
Jerusalem, Kreuzritterzeit,
12. Jahrhundert n. Chr., Diameter 4,5 cm

Siegeldruck des Amalricus de Nesle, des neunten
Lateinischen Patriarchen Jerusalems. Vorderseite: eine fünfreihige Inschrift
«Amalricus Sanctae Resurrectionis Ecclesiae Patriarcha»;
Rückseite: eine Darstellung von Christus in der Vorhölle als Zeichen
der Wiederauferstehung.

בולה מעופרת
ירושלים, תקופת הצלבנים, המאה הי"ב לסה"נ, קוטר 4.5 ס"מ

טביעת־חותם של אמלריקוס דה נסלה, הפטריארך הלטיני התשיעי של ירושלים.
לפנים: כתובת לטינית בת חמש שורות: Amalricus Sanctae Resurrectionis Ecclesiae Patriarcha
גב: תיאור תחייתו של ישו.

IV

Neighbouring and Distant Cultures

The great civilizations of Egypt and the countries of the Levant.
Their influence on the utilitarian objects and art works of the country through trade,
wars and occupation.
Arts of non-Western civilizations: interpretative, non-mimetic representation of reality in Africa,
Oceania, and pre-Columbian, Indian and Eskimo America.
The spectrum of Asian art, from the exuberance of Indian sculpture to
the serenity of Chinese ceramics.

Cultures voisines et éloignées

Les grandes civilisations d'Egypte et des pays du Levant.
Leur influence sur les objets usuels et les œuvres d'art de ce pays au travers
du commerce, des guerres et des occupations.
Les arts des civilisations non occidentales: incarnation interprétative et non mimétique de la réalité
en Afrique, Océanie et l'Amérique pré-Colombienne, Indienne et Eskimo.
L'éventail de l'art asiatique, de l'exubérance de la sculpture indienne
à la sérénité de la céramique chinoise.

Nachbarländer und ferne Kulturen

Die großen Zivilisationen Ägyptens und der Levante.
Ihr Einfluß auf Gebrauchsgegenstände und Kunstwerke dieses Landes durch Handel,
Kriege und Besetzung.
Kunst der Außereuropäischen Zivilisationen: die interpretierende aber nicht
imitierende Verkörperung der Realität in Afrika, Ozeanien und bei den präkolumbischen,
indianischen und Eskimo Völkern Amerikas.
Das Spektrum der asiatischen Kunst von der Fülle indischer Skulpturen bis zur
edlen Einfachheit chinesischer Keramik reichend.

תרבויות שכנות ורחוקות

התרבויות הגדולות של מצרים ומערב-אסיה.
השפעותיהן על כלי יום-יום וחפצי אמנות בארץ-ישראל באמצעות מסחר, מלחמות וכיבוש.
תרבויות שאינן מערביות: ייצוג המציאות שלא בדרך החיקוי
באפריקה, באוקיאניה, באמריקה הקדם-קולומביאנית ובקרב האינדיאנים והאסקימואים של אמריקה. קשת האמנות
האסיאתית – מן החיוניות של הפיסול ההודי ועד לקרמיקה הסינית השלווה והמאופקת.

SMITING GOD ON LION
Syria, second millennium BCE, h. 15 cm

This bronze statuette depicts the storm god called Hadad
by the Canaanites or Teshub in the Hittite
language. He is symbolized both by the smiting god posture and
by his animal attribute.

LE DIEU HADAD DRESSÉ SUR UN LION
Syrie, IIe millénaire av. l'ère chrétienne, h. 15 cm

Image en bronze du dieu de l'orage,
appelé Hadad par les Cananéens et Teshub en langue
hittite. Il est symbolisé par la posture du dieu prêt à frapper et l'attribut
animal qui l'accompagne.

DER GOTT HADAD AUF EINEM LÖWEN STEHEND
Syrien, 2. Jahrtausend v. Chr., H. 15 cm

Diese Statuette aus Bronze zeigt
den Sturmgott, der von den Kanaaniten Hadad und in hethitischer
Sprache Teschub genannt wurde. Er ist sinnbildlich durch die Haltung des
«Schlagenden Gottes» und sein Tierattribute dargestellt.

אל מכה ניצב על אריה
סוריה, האלף השני לפסה"נ, ג' 15 ס"מ

פסלון ברונזה זה של אל הסערה – "הדד" בפי הכנענים או "תשוב" בפי החיתים – מאופיין בתנוחת הגוף
של אל מכה ובאריה המשויך לו.

LIMESTONE MOURNER STATUETTE
Egypt, 23rd-20th century BCE, h. 7.8 cm

In Old Kingdom illustrations,
women mourners of this type are depicted as riding in funerary boats
on either side of the coffin.

FIGURINE DE PLEUREUSE EN CALCAIRE
Egypte, XXIIIe-XXe siècle av. l'ère chrétienne, h. 7,8 cm

Dans les illustrations datant de
l'Ancien Empire, des pleureuses de ce genre figurent de part et d'autre
du cercueil dans les barques funèbres.

KALKSTEINSTATUETTE EINER TRAUENDEN
Ägypten, 23.-20. Jahrhundert v. Chr., H. 7,8 cm

In Illustrationen aus dem Alten Reich
sind trauende Frauen dieses Typs in Bestattungsbooten auf beiden Seiten
des Sarges sitzend dargestellt.

פסלון מקוננת מאבן־גיר
מצרים. המאות הכ״ג-הכ׳ לפסה״נ, ג 7.8 ס״מ

באיורים מתקופת הממלכה הקדומה תוארו מקוננות מטיפוס זה כשהן יושבות בסירות־לוויה משני צדי
ארון המת.

ELECTRUM PLAQUE WITH WINGED NUDE FEMALE
Syria or Anatolia, 8th-7th century BCE, h. 7.2 cm

The figure, holding bunches of grapes, is probably the goddess of wine.
The plaque, which may have formed part of a crown, is worked in a variety of
techniques, including colourful inlays now lost.

FEMME AILÉE SUR PLAQUE D'ÉLECTRUM
Syrie ou Anatolie, VIIIᵉ-VIIᵉ siècle av. l'ère chrétienne, h. 7,2 cm

Image de femme tenant une grappe de raisins dans chaque main –
probablement la déesse du vin. La plaque, qui faisait peut-être partie
d'une couronne, est travaillée dans diverses techniques qui comprenaient
à l'origine des incrustations colorées.

ELECTRIUM-PLÄTTCHEN MIT GEFLÜGELTER WEIBLICHER FIGUR
Syrien oder Anatolia, 8.-7. Jahrhundert v. Chr., H. 7,2 cm

Die Figur, die Weintrauben hält, stellt vermutlich die Göttin des Weines dar.
Das Plättchen das Teil einer Krone gewesen sein mag ist in
verschiedenen Techniken ausgeführt, darunter auch inzwischen
verlorengegangenen Farbintarsien.

לוחית אלקטרום ועליה דמות עירומה מכונפת
סוריה או אנטוליה, המאה הח'-הז' לפסה"נ. ג. 7.2 ס"מ

הדמות, המחזיקה אשכולות ענבים, היא כנראה אלת יין. הלוחית, שהיתה אולי חלק מכתר, מעובדת
במגוון של טכניקות, בהן שיבוץ אבנים צבעוניות (לא שרדו).

PAINTED POTTERY KYLIX
Cyprus, 7th century BCE, h. 15 cm

The scene of birds flanking a lotus flower, depicted on
both sides of the vase, is a fine example of the bichrome technique which
prevailed in the Cypro-Archaic period.

KYLIX DE TERRE CUITE PEINT
Chypre, VIIᵉ siècle av. l'ère chrétienne, h. 15 cm

Le motif d'oiseaux entourant une
fleur de lotus est répété sur l'autre face du vase qui est un bel exemple
de poterie bichrome de la période chypriote-archaïque.

BEMALTES TON-KYLIX
Zypern, 7. Jahrhundert v. Chr., H. 15 cm

Eine Vogelszene zu Seiten einer Lotusblume ist auf beiden Hälften
der Vase dargestellt. Dies ist ein schönes Beispiel für die Zweifarbentechnik,
die in der zyprisch-archaischen Zeit vorherrschte.

גביע חרס מצויר
קפריסין. המאה ה7' לפסה"נ. ג 15 ס"מ

את שני צדי הגביע מעטרת תמונת ציפורים משני עברי פרח לוטוס. זוהי דוגמה נאה ביותר לסגנון הציור
שרווח בתקופה הקיפרו־ארכאית.

BRONZE HYDRIA
Greek, 425 BCE, h. 44 cm

A sumptuous vessel with a figure of a harpy on one of its three handles.

HYDRIE DE BRONZE
Grèce, 425 av. l'ère chrétienne, h. 44 cm

Magnifique vase orné de la figure d'une harpie sur l'une des trois anses.

BRONZE HYDRIA
Griechisch, 425 v. Chr., H. 44 cm

Ein prächtiges Gefäß mit drei Henkeln. Auf einem der Henkel
ist eine Harpyie dargestellt.

הידריה מברונזה
יוון. 425 לפסה"נ. ג. 44 ס"מ

כלי מפואר בעל שלוש ידיות ועל אחת מהן דמות הרפייה.

GELEDE MASK
Yoruba, Nigeria, 32 x 17 x 20 cm

This wooden mask was worn in rites of the
Gelede secret society, to honour and appease the awesome
witchcraft activities of elderly women.

MASQUE GELEDE
Yorouba, Nigéria, 32 x 17 x 20 cm

Masque de bois porté dans les rites de la
société secrète Gelede en l'honneur des femmes âgées et pour conjurer
les maléfices de leurs pratiques de sorcellerie.

GELEDE MASKE
Yoruba, Nigeria, 32 x 17 x 20 cm

Diese Holzmaske wurde während der Riten der Gelede
Geheimgesellschaft getragen, um die Wirkung der furchterregenden
Hexereien der alten Frauen zu mildern.

מסכת גלדה
יורובה, ניגריה, 32×17×20 ס"מ

מסכת עץ זו היו עוטים בטקסי גלדה (חבורת סתרים) כדי לרצות את זקנות השבט ולהתגונן בפני
כשפיהן.

TWO WOMEN HOLDING BIRDS
China, Tang dynasty,
early 17th century, h. 37 cm

While clearly female, these figurines of glazed
earthenware wear male dress, which was not uncommon
during the Tang period.

DEUX FEMMES TENANT DES OISEAUX
Chine, dynastie Tang, début du XVIIe siècle,
terre cuite vernie, h. 37 cm

Bien que visiblement elles représentent
des femmes, ces figurines portent des vêtements d'homme –
ce qui était assez courant pendant la période Tang.

ZWEI FRAUEN MIT VÖGELN
China, Tang Dynastie,
frühes 17. Jahrhundert, H. 37 cm

Obwohl die Figuren aus glasiertem Ton deutlich
Frauen darstellen, tragen sie männliche Kleidung, was während
der Tang Periode nicht ungewöhnlich war.

שתי נשים אוחזות ציפורים
סין, שושלת טאנג, ראשית המאה הח', ג 37 ס"מ

דמויות הנשים, העשויות חרס מזוגג, מוצגות בבגדי גברים, תופעה שלא היתה חריגה בתקופת טאנג.

SHIVA
India, Uttar Pradesh, c. 5th-6th century CE,
Terracotta, h. 38 cm

This part of a larger terracotta relief is representative of the bold and
expressive reliefs of the Gupta period.

SHIVA
Inde, Uttar Pradesh, V^e-VIe siècle,
terracotta, h. 38 cm

Fragment d'un relief d'argile; il représente bien les reliefs expressifs
de la période Gupta.

SHIVA
Indien, Uttar Pradesh, um 5.-6. Jahrhundert,
Terracotta, H. 38 cm

Dieser Teil eines größeren Terracotta-Reliefs ist typisch für die klaren
und ausdrucksvollen Reliefs der Gupta Periode.

האל שיווה

הודו, אוטאר פראדש, המאות הה׳-הו׳, ג 38 ס״מ

חלק זה מתבליט חרס גדול מאפיין את התבליטים עזי-ההבעה מתקופת גופטה.

BRIDAL ATTIRE
San'a, Yemen, late 19th - early 20th century,
gilt silver, pearls, corals

Reconstructed outfit of the
Jewesses of San'a, consisting of a pearl crown, multiple necklaces, bracelets
and rings, a brocade coat and silk veil.
The bride was attired by a special "bride-dresser" who lent
the costume for the occasion.

TENUE DE MARIÉE
Sanaa, Yémen, fin du XIXᵉ siècle - début du XXᵉ siècle,
argent doré, perles fines, corail

Vêtement reconstitué porté par les Juives de Sanaa.
Il comprend un diadème de perles fines, de multiples colliers, bracelets et bagues,
un manteau de brocart et un voile de soie.
La mariée était parée par une habilleuse qui prêtait le costume
pour la cérémonie du mariage.

BRAUTGEWAND
San'a, Jemen, spätes 19. Jahrhundert - frühes 20. Jahrhundert,
vergoldetes Silber, Silber, Perlen, Korallen, Brokat, Seide

Rekonstruierte Tracht der Jüdinnen
von San'a, bestehend aus einer Perlenkrone, verschiedenartigen Halsketten,
Armbändern und Ringen, einem Brokatmantel und Seidentuch. Die Braut wurde
von einer speziellen «Braut-Ankleidefrau» geschmückt,
von der die gesamte Tracht für diese Gelegenheit ausgeliehen wurde.

לבוש כלה

צנעא, תימן, סוף המאה הי"ט-ראשית המאה הכ׳, כסף מוזהב, פנינים ואלמוגים

לבוש משוחזר של כלה יהודיה, הכולל מעיל ברוקאד וצעיף משי, וכן נזר פנינים, ענקים, צמידים
וטבעות. לבוש זה היה שייך למלבישה, והיא שהשאילה אותו לכלה והלבישה אותה בו.

GREAT NECKLACE OF THE JEWESSES OF SAN'A
San'a, Yemen, late 19th century - early 20th century,
silver, gilt, filigree work

Necklaces like this made by Jewish
silversmiths, were worn by the bride round the chin during the wedding ceremony
and later by married women as a pectoral on festive occasions.

COLLIER D'APPARAT DES JUIVES DE SANAA
Sanaa, Yémen, fin du XIXe siècle - début du XXe siècle,
argent, dorure, filigrane

Ces colliers – l'œuvre d'artisans juifs – étaient portés par les
femmes autour du menton le jour du mariage; par la suite, elles les portaient
en collier dans les grandes occasions.

GROSSES HALSGESCHMEIDE GETRAGEN VON JÜDINNEN IN SAN'A
San'a, Jemen, spätes 19. Jahrhundert - frühes 20. Jahrhundert,
vergoldetes Silber, Filigranarbeit

Solcher Halsschmuck, von jüdischen Silberschmieden
hergestellt, wurde von der Braut während der Hochzeit auf dem Kinn getragen.
Später trug ihn die verheiratete Frau zu festlichen Anlässen als Kette.

ענק נשים יהודיות מצנעא
צנעא. תימן. סוף המאה הי״ט-ראשית המאה הכ׳. כסף מוזהב. עבודת פיליגראן

ענקים מסוג זה. שנעשו בידי צורפים יהודיים. ענדו כלות מסביב לסנטרן בעת החתונה ואחר-כך.
בהזדמנויות חגיגיות. מסביב לצוואר.

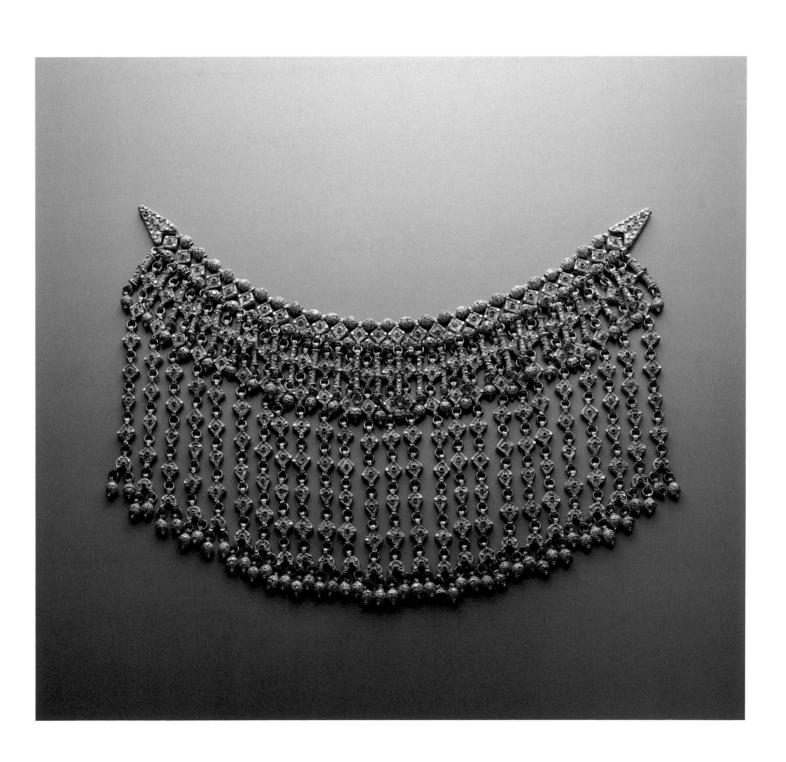

BRIDAL AND CEREMONIAL COSTUME
Tetouan, Morocco, 19th century, velvet, metal-thread
embroidery, lace and brocade

This costume, which originated in the Spanish Renaissance
court dresses, was brought to Morocco by the Jews who fled the Inquisition.
Over the centuries, it became their distinctive wear.

COSTUME NUPTIAL ET DE CÉRÉMONIE
Tétouan, Maroc, XIXᵉ siècle, velours, broderies d'or
et d'argent, dentelle, brocart

Ce costume qui tire son origine des robes de
cour de la Renaissance espagnole, fut amené au Maroc par les Juifs fuyant l'Inquisition.
Avec le temps, il devint le costume traditionnel des juives marocaines.

BRAUT- UND FESTGEWAND
Tetouan, Marokko, 19. Jahrhundert, Samt,
Metallfadenstickerei, Spitze und Brokat

Dieses Kostüm, das seinen Ursprung in den spanischen
Hofgewändern der Renaissance hat, wurde von Juden, die vor der Inquisition flohen
nach Marokko gebracht. Im Laufe der Jahrhunderte
wurde es zur typischen Tracht der marokkanischen Jüdinnen.

לבוש טקס לאשה

טטואן, מארוקו, המאה הי״ט. קטיפה, רקמת חוט מתכת וסרטים מוזהבים

תלבושת זו, שמקורה בשמלת חצר־המלכות בספרד בתקופת הרנסאנס, הובאה למארוקו בידי פליטי
האינקוויזיציה. במרוצת השנים הפכה להיות תלבושת ייחודית ליהודיות.

TWO NECKLACES
Morocco, early 20th century, silver, coins, corals,
semi-precious stones and enamel

Typical of jewellery worn
by the Jewish women of the Sous region in the
Atlas mountains; the cloisonné enamel was common in Jewish
workmanship of this region.

DEUX COLLIERS
Maroc, début du XXe siècle, argent, monnaies,
corail, pierres semi-précieuses, émail

Exemples typiques des bijoux
portés par les Juives dans les montagnes de l'Atlas de la
région du Sous. A noter que l'émail cloisonné figure souvent dans le travail
des artisans juifs de cette région.

ZWEI HALSKETTEN
Marokko, frühes 20. Jahrhundert, Silber, Münzen,
Korallen, Halbedelsteine und Email

Typisch für den Schmuck, der von jüdischen Frauen in der Gegend von
Sous im Atlasgebirge getragen wurde.
Cloisonné-Emailarbeit gehörte zum jüdischen Kunsthandwerk
dieser Gegend.

שני ענקי נשים
מארוקו. ראשית המאה הכ׳. כסף. מטבעות. אלמוגים. אבנים יקרות-למחצה ואמאייל

עדיים אלה אופייניים לנשים יהודיות באזור סוס שבהרי האטלס. עבודת האמאייל והקלאוזונה טיפוסית
לאומנים יהודיים באזורים אלו.

WINDOW IN LATTICEWORK
Morocco, 20th century, wood, carved and painted

Decorated windows like this were common in Moroccan homes.
They made it possible to look out without being seen and formed an important
element in interior design.

MOUCHARABIEH
Maroc, XXᵉ siècle, bois sculpté et peint

Des fenêtres garnies de bois
sculpté en treillis, comme celle-ci, étaient courantes au Maroc. Elles permettaient
de voir sans être vu et figuraient en bonne place dans la décoration
intérieure des maisons.

GITTERFENSTER
Marokko, 20. Jahrhundert, Holz, geschnitzt und bemalt

Solche dekorierten Fenster waren in
marokkanischen Häusern üblich. Sie machten es möglich, aus dem Fenster zu
schauen, ohne gesehen zu werden und waren zugleich ein wichtiges
Element der Innendekoration.

חלון מעשה סבכה
מארוקו. המאה הכ'. עץ מגולף וצבוע

חלונות מעוטרים כאלה היו נפוצים בבתי מארוקו. הם איפשרו לבני-הבית לראות את הנעשה בחוץ בלא
שייראו בעצמם. והיו מרכיב חשוב בעיצוב פנים הבית.

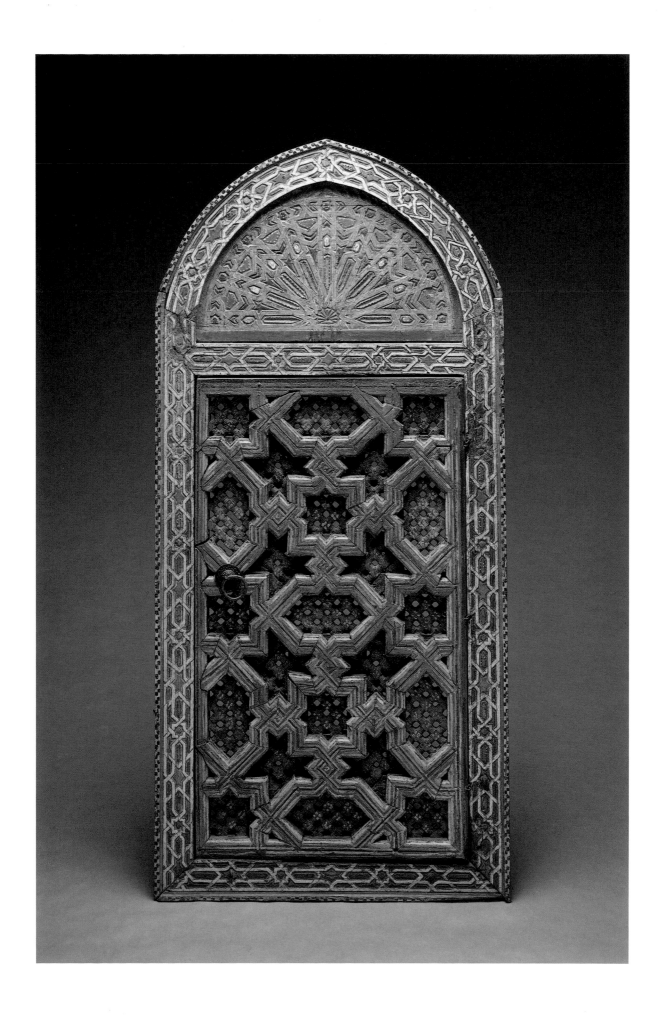

COAT FOR BAR-MITZVAH BOY
Bokhara, 19th century, fabric covered with
silk thread embroidery

Festive coats were usually made of colourful, ikat-dyed,
silks, or of velvet embroidered with gold and silk. This coat is one of the
few surviving specimens of its type.

COSTUME DE BAR-MITZVAH
Boukhara, XIXᵉ siècle, le tissu est entièrement
brodé de soie

Les vêtements de fêtes étaient couramment de soie de
couleurs vives ou de velours brodé d'or et de soie. Le manteau de jeune
garçon vu ici est une pièce rare.

MANTEL FÜR DEN BAR-MITZVAH-JUNGEN
Buchara, 19. Jahrhundert,
Stoff mit Seidenfadenstickerei bedeckt

Festliche Mäntel wurden im allgemeinen aus bunten
Seidenstoffen oder aus mit Seide und Gold
besticktem Samt hergestellt. Dieser Mantel, mit seiner außerordentlich feinen
Stickerei ist ein seltenes Exemplar.

מעיל לנער בר-מצוה

בוכארה, המאה הי״ט, אריג פשתן מכוסה רקמת חוטי משי

מעילים חגיגיים נעשו בדרך כלל מאריגי איקט משי צבעוניים, או מאריגי קטיפה שעליהם רקמו בחוטי
משי וזהב. מעיל מכוסה ברקמה עדינה כגון זה נדיר ביותר.

ADORNMENT FOR FOREHEAD OR FRONT OF CAP
Bokhara, 19th century, gold and semi-precious stones

The most typical of the resplendent Bokhara jewellery worn by urban women
in Uzbekistan till the 1920's. Its value was determined by
the number, length and quality of the tourmaline and white pearl
hangings and by the thickness of the
gold leaf in which the precious stones were set.

ORNEMENT DE FRONT OU GARNITURE DE BONNET
Boukhara, XIXᵉ siècle, or, pierres semi-précieuses

Le plus typique parmi les bijoux
resplendissants dont se paraient les citadines de l'Uzbékistan
jusqu'aux années 20. Sa valeur dépendait du nombre de pendants, de leur longueur
et de la qualité des perles de tourmaline et des
perles fines qui les composaient, ainsi que de l'épaisseur de la feuille
d'or dans laquelle les pierres étaient serties.

KOPFSCHMUCK, AUF DER STIRN ODER KAPPE ZU TRAGEN
Buchara, 19. Jahrhundert, Gold und Halbedelsteine

Ein typisches Beispiel für den prächtigen
bucharischen Schmuck, der in Uzbekistan bis in die zwanziger Jahre
von Stadtfrauen getragen wurde. Der Wert wurde durch
die Anzahl, Länge und Qualität
der Turmalin- und Perlengehänge bestimmt und durch die Dicke des
Blattgoldes, in das die Steine gefaßt waren.

עיטור למצח או לכיפת אשה
בוכארה, המאה הי״ט, זהב ואבנים יקרות־למחצה

תכשיט זה אופייני ביותר לתכשיטי בוכארה המפוארים וענדו אותו נשים עירוניות באוזבקיסתאן עד
שנות העשרים של מאה זו. ערכו היה נקבע על־פי הפנינים והטורמלינים התלויים עליו - מספרם, אורכם
ואיכותם - וכן על־פי עובי הזהב שבו שובצו.

EMBROIDERED WALL-HANGING
Bokhara, 18th century, linen, silk thread

Wall hangings were a traditional
decoration in homes, courts of rulers and mosques.
They served Jews in synagogues as Torah ark curtains and were
used in the booths of Sukkot.

TENTURE BRODÉE
Boukhara, XVIIIᵉ siècle, soie sur toile de lin

Les tentures servaient d'ornement
traditionnel dans les maisons, les palais, les mosquées. Les Juifs
les utilisaient dans les synagogues comme rideau pour l'Arche de la Torah
ou encore pour orner les cabanes de Souccot.

BESTICKTER WANDBEHANG
Buchara, 18. Jahrhundert, Leinen, Seidenfaden

Traditionelle Dekoration in Privathäusern, Schlössern
und Moscheen. Von Juden als Thoraschreinvorhänge in Synagogen und
am Sukkothfest in den Laubhütten benützt.

יריעת פאר רקומה
בוכארה, המאה הי״ח, פשתן, חוטי משי

יריעות רקומות היו עיטור קיר מסורתי בבתים, בחצרות שליטים ובמסגדים. ליהודים שימשו בבתי־כנסת
כפרוכות וכן לקישוט סוכה.

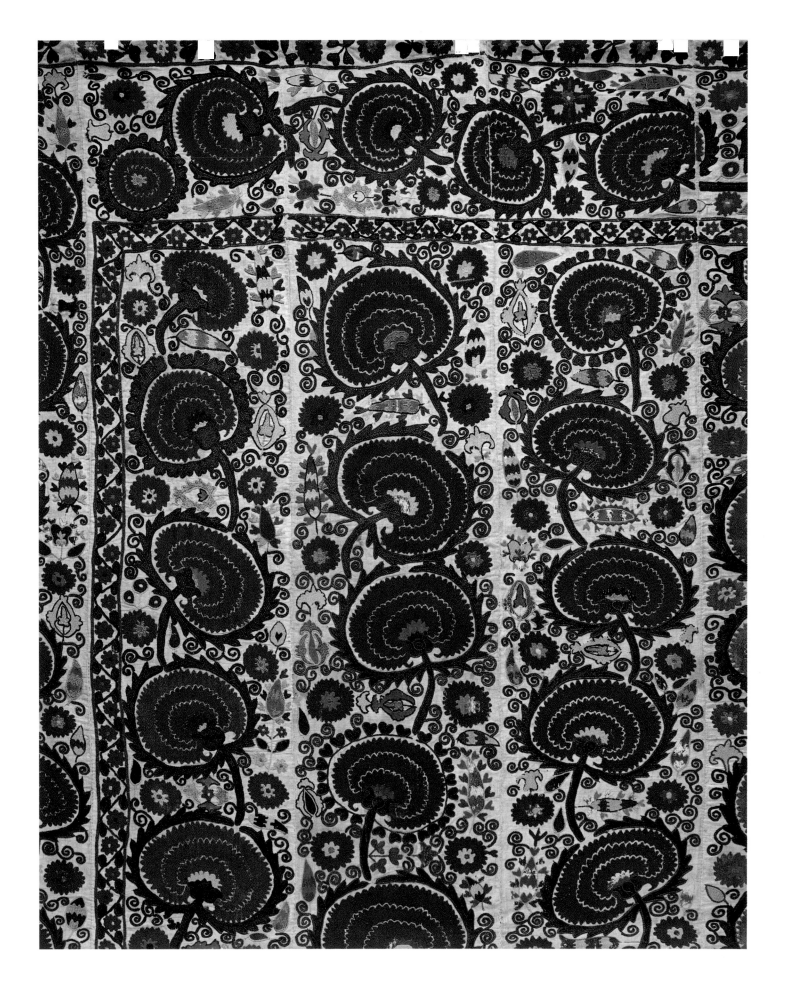

EMBROIDERED CHEST PANEL OF WOMAN'S DRESS
Beth-Jallah, Bethlehem region, 1930,
silk fabric, coloured silk thread, metal cords

This chest panel is typical of
the highly developed Bethlehem embroidery. It belongs
to the *ahdari* type dress, first used as a wedding attire and afterwards as
a ceremonial and festive costume.

PLASTRON DE ROBE BRODÉ
Beth-Jallah, région de Bethléem, 1930, tissu, fils de soie
de couleurs, cordonnet de métal

Ce panneau de corsage est un bel exemple de la broderie de Bethléem
où cet art est hautement développé. Il fait partie du type
ahdari qui, d'abord robe de mariée, devient ensuite costume porté
lors des cérémonies et des jours des fêtes.

BESTICKTER BRUSTEINSATZ EINES FRAUENGEWANDES
Beth-Jallah, Bethlehem Gegend, 1930,
Seidenstoff, farbiger Seidenfaden, Metallschnüre

Dieser Brusteinsatz ist typisch
für die hochentwickelte Bethlehem-Stickerei. Es gehört zu dem
Ahdari-Kleid, das zuerst als Hochzeitskleid, später dann als zeremonielles
und festliches Gewand getragen wird.

לבבית רקומה לשמלת אשה

בית־ג׳אלה, 1930. אריג משי רקום בחוטי משי צבעוניים ובפתילי מתכת

לבבית זו עשויה בסגנון הרקמה המפוארת של בית־לחם. היא שייכת לשמלת "אח'דארי", ששימשה
לאשה תחילה כשמלת חתונה ואח"כ לחגים וטקסים.

VI

Judaica

Ceremonial objects used by Jews in the synagogue and at home throughout the Jewish year.
Their formal and functional unity, and the stylistic diversity reflecting
the impact of the host cultures.

Judaïca

Les objets de cérémonie accompagnant le juif à la synagogue et chez soi tout au long de l'année juive.
Leur unité formelle et fonctionnelle, leur diversité stylistique reflétant
l'empreinte de l'environnement culturel.

Judaica

Kultgeräte für Synagoge und Haus, die das jüdische Jahr begleiten.
Ihre formale und funktionelle Einheitlichkeit bei stilistischer Mannigfaltigkeit,
die die Kulturen der Gastländer widerspiegelt.

אמנות יהודית

תשמישי מצווה וקדושה ליוו את היהודי במחזור חייו ובחגים, בבית ובבית־כנסת.
אחדות הצורה והתכלית שלהם לצד הגיוון הסגנוני, המשקף את שלל התרבויות שבתוכן נוצרו.

BIRDS' HEAD HAGGADAH
Southern Germany, c. 1300,
illuminated manuscript on vellum, 27 x 18.5 cm

The phenomenon of animal and bird-headed human figures in
medieval Ashkenazi manuscripts might have derived from the problematic aspect of
the depictions of the human face in Judaism.

LA HAGGADAH À TÊTES D'OISEAUX
Allemagne du Sud, env. 1300,
manuscrit enluminé sur vélin, 27 x 18,5 cm

La représentation de personnages à têtes d'oiseaux, ou
d'animaux, dans certains manuscrits ashkénazes du moyen-âge est sans doute dû
aux problèmes posés par la figuration humaine dans le Judaïsme.

VOGELKOPF HAGGADAH
Süddeutschland, um 1300, illuminierte Handschrift
auf Pergament, 27 x 18,5 cm

Die Darstellung von Menschen mit Tier- oder Vogelköpfen in
mittelalterlichen aschkenasischen Handschriften hat möglicherweise ihren Ursprung
in der religiösen Problematik die die Wiedergabe des menschlichen
Gesichts dem Judentum bedeutet.

הגדת ראשי הציפורים
דרום־גרמניה, 1300 בקירוב, כתב־יד מעוטר על קלף, 27 × 18.5 ס"מ

התופעה של עיוות הדמות האנושית וציור דמויות אדם בעלות פני חיה או ציפור בכתבי־יד אשכנזיים
מימי־הביניים נובעת כנראה מן הבעייתיות של תיאור פני אדם ביהדות.

DE CASTRO PENTATEUCH
Germany, 1344, illuminated manuscript on vellum,
46 x 31 cm

The page reproduced here is the opening of the
Book of Deuteronomy. Similar initial-word panels appear at the beginning
of each of the other four books.

LE PENTATEUQUE DE DE CASTRO
Allemagne, 1344, manuscrit enluminé sur vélin,
46 x 31 cm

La page reproduite ici est le commencement du Deutéronome.
Les premières pages des autres livres du Pentateuque sont ornées comme celle-ci d'un
panneau décoratif dans lequel s'inscrit le premier mot.

DE CASTRO PENTATEUCH
Deutschland, 1344, illuminierte Handschrift auf Pergament,
46 x 31 cm

Diese Seite zeigt den Anfang des Buches Deuteronomium
(5. Buch Mosis). Eine ähnliche ornamentale Initialwort-Tafel erscheint am Anfang
jedes Buches des Pentateuchs.

חומש דה קאסטרו
גרמניה, שנת ק"ד (1344). כתב־יד מעוטר על קלף. 46 × 31 ס"מ

הדף המצולם הוא דף הפתיחה לספר דברים. מלות־פתיחה מעוטרות דומות מופיעות בראשיתו של כל
אחד מהספרים האחרים שבכתב־היד.

THE ROTHSCHILD MISCELLANY
Northern Italy, 1470-1480,
illuminated manuscript on vellum, 21 x 15.9 cm

This splendid manuscript contains about seventy books, including biblical,
liturgical, historical and philosophical treatises. It has about two hundred illustrations
and hundreds of decorated initial-word panels.

LE MANUSCRIT ROTHSCHILD
Italie du Nord, 1470-1480,
manuscrit enluminé sur vélin, 21 x 15,9 cm

Cette œuvre somptueuse comprend environ soixante-dix ouvrages ayant trait à
la Bible, la liturgie, l'histoire et la philosophie. Elle est enrichie de près de deux cents
enluminures, sans compter plusieurs centaines d'en-têtes richement décorés.

DAS ROTHSCHILD MANUSKRIPT
Norditalien, 1470-1480,
illuminierte Handschrift auf Pergament, 21 x 15,9 cm

Diese prächtige Bilderhandschrift enthält ungefähr siebzig Bücher, darunter
biblische, liturgische, historische und philosophische Abhandlungen.
Etwa zweihundert Illustrationen und Hunderte von illuminierten Initialwort Tafeln
schmücken die Handschrift.

כתב־יד רוטשילד

צפון־איטליה, 1470-1480, כתב־יד מצויר על קלף, 21×15.9 ס"מ

כתב־יד מפואר זה כולל כשבעים חיבורים שונים, ביניהם ספרי התנ"ך, ספרי תפילה, היסטוריה,
פילוסופיה ומוסר. הוא מכיל כמאתיים איורים לטקסט וכן מאות מלות־פתיחה מעוטרות.

TORAH ARK
Northern Italy, 1701, carved and gilt
A Torah ark from the baroque synagogue of Vittorio Veneto which was transferred
in its entirety and installed in the Israel Museum.

ARCHE DE TORAH
Italie du Nord, 1701, bois sculpté et dorures
Fait partie de la synagogue baroque de Vittorio Veneto qui a été transportée en Israël
et entièrement reconstituée au Musée.

THORASCHREIN
Norditalien, 1701, Holz, geschnitzt und vergoldet
Aus der barocken Synagoge von Vittorio Veneto, die als Ganzes ins Israel Museum
überführt und dort wiedererrichtet wurde.

ארון קודש
צפון־איטליה, תס״א (1701), עץ מגולף ומוזהב

מתוך בית־הכנסת מתקופת הבארוק של ויטוריו ונטו, אשר הועבר בשלמותו והותקן במוזיאון ישראל.

SYNAGOGUE
Horb (near Bamberg), Southern Germany, 1735

The ceiling and walls of this now rare specimen of a wooden synagogue,
were painted by Eliezer Susmann, originally from Brody, Poland. The decoration is
similar in style to Polish painted wooden synagogues.

SYNAGOGUE
Horb (près de Bamberg), Allemagne du Sud, 1735

Le plafond et les parois de cette synagogue de bois, d'un type désormais très rare,
ont été peints par Eliézer Susmann, natif de Brody en Pologne.
La décoration est semblable à celle des synagogues de bois polonaises.

SYNAGOGE
Horb (in der Nähe von Bamberg), Süddeutschland, 1735

Die Decke und Wände dieser Holzsynagoge, heute eine große Seltenheit,
wurden von Elizer Susmann bemalt, der aus Brody in Polen stammte. Die Dekoration ist
im Stil der ehemals zahlreichen bemalten polnischen Holzsynagogen.

בית־כנסת
הורב (ליד במברג), דרום־גרמניה, 1735. עץ צבוע

התקרה והקירות של בית־כנסת זה - אולי היחיד ששרד בסוגו - צוירו בידי אליעזר זוסמן ב"ר שלמה כץ
מבראד (פולין). ואכן, העיטורים דומים בסגנונם לעיטורי בתי־כנסת פולניים מעץ.

KETUBAH (MARRIAGE CONTRACT)
Rotterdam, Netherlands, 1648,
manuscript and coloured etching on parchment, 48 x 39 cm

The frame was decorated by Shalom Italia (c. 1619-c. 1655), a Jewish engraver
especially famous for his *megillot* (Scrolls of Esther) engravings.

KETOUBAH (CONTRAT DE MARIAGE)
Rotterdam, Hollande, 1648,
manuscrit et estampe colorée sur parchemin, 48 x 39 cm

L'encadrement décoratif est de Shalom Italia, un graveur juif (env. 1619-env. 1655),
réputé pour ses *méguilot* (Rouleaux du Livre d'Esther).

KETUBAH (HEIRATSVERTRAG)
Rotterdam, Niederlande, 1648,
Handschrift und farbige Radierung auf Pergament, 48 x 39 cm

Die Umrandung stammt von Shalom Italia (ca. 1619-ca. 1655), einem jüdischen
Kupferstecher, berühmt durch seine mit Stichen verzierten *Megillot* (Estherrollen).

כתובה

רוטרדאם, הולנד, 1648, כתב־יד ותחריט צבוע על קלף, 48 × 39 ס"מ

עיטורי המסגרת נעשו בידי שלום איטליה (1655-1619 בקירוב), מפתח־נחושת יהודי שנתפרסם במיוחד
במעטר מגילות אסתר.

TORAH CASES

Right: India, 19th century (?), painted wood; *rimonim:* Yemen, 19th-20th century, brass
Left: Iran, 1874, wood, cotton and silver; *rimonim:* Iran, 19th century, silver

Among the Oriental communities, the Torah scroll is kept within a wooden case (tiq),
often painted or decorated by metal plaques.

ETUIS À TORAH

A droite: Inde, XIXᵉ siècle (?), bois peint; *rimonim:* Yémen, XIXᵉ-XXᵉ siècle, laiton
A gauche: Iran, 1874, bois, coton et argent; *rimonim,* XIXᵉ siècle, argent

Dans certaines communautés juives orientales, le Rouleau de la Torah est enfermé
dans des boîtes en bois, souvent peintes ou ornées de plaques de métal.

THORAKASTEN

Rechts: Indien, 19. Jahrhundert (?), bemaltes Holz;
Rimonim: Jemen, 19.-20. Jahrhundert, Messing
Links: Iran, 1874, Holz, Baumwollstoff und Silber; *Rimonim:* Iran, 19. Jahrhundert, Silber

In orientalischen jüdischen Gemeinden wird die Thorarolle in einem Holzkasten
(tik) aufbewahrt, der oft bemalt oder mit Metallbeschlägen verziert ist.

תיקים לספר תורה

מימין: הודו, המאה הי״ט (?), עץ צבוע; הרימונים: תימן, המאה הי״ט-כ׳, פליז
משמאל: איראן, 1874, עץ, אריג כותנה וכסף; הרימונים: איראן, המאה הי״ט, כסף

בקהילות המזרח מקובל להחזיק את ספר התורה בתיק מעץ, המעוטר לעתים קרובות בצביעה או מקושט
בלוחיות מתכת.

HANUKKAH LAMP
Germany, 18th century, silver, partly gilt

This hanukkah lamp is particularly noteworthy for its elaborate
ornamentation, consisting of tiny animal depictions and human figures including Moses
and Aaron, Judah Macabee, and Judith holding the head of Holofernes.

LAMPE DE HANOUCAH
Allemagne, XVIIIᵉ siècle, argent en partie doré

Cette lampe de Hanoucah est particulièrement remarquable par son
ornementation élaborée qui consiste en figures animales et humaines minuscules,
dont Moïse, Aaron, Judah Maccabée, et Judith tenant la tête de Holopherne.

CHANUKKA-LAMPE
Deutschland, 18. Jahrhundert, Silber, teilweise vergoldet

Chanukka-Lampe, besonders bemerkenswert wegen ihrer reichen
Ausschmückung. Diese besteht aus winzigen Tier- und Menschen-Darstellungen, darunter
Moses und Aaron, Judah Makkabäus und Judith, den Kopf des Holofernes haltend.

מנורת חנוכה
גרמניה, המאה הי״ח, כסף מוזהב בחלקו

מנורה מפוארת זו מצטיינת בשפע עיטוריה, הכוללים דמויות חיות ואדם, בהם דמות משה ואהרן, יהודה
המכבי, ויהודית אוחזת בראש הולופרנס.

SPICE-BOXES
From right to left: Brno, Moravia, 1872-1922;
Germany (?), 19th century; Berlin, early 19th century;
Poland, 18th-19th century; Germany, 19th century

In Europe, tower shaped spice-boxes, usually made of silver, were often used
for the ritual of smelling spices on the termination of the Sabbath.

BOÎTES À AROMATES
De droite à gauche: Brno, Moravie, 1872-1922;
Allemagne (?), XIXᵉ siècle; Berlin, début du XIXᵉ siècle;
Pologne, XVIIIᵉ-XIXᵉ siècle; Allemagne, XIXᵉ siècle

Les épices dont on respire le parfum au cours de la cérémonie
marquant la fin du Sabbat étaient généralement conservées, en Europe, dans
des boîtes souvent en argent en forme de tours.

GEWÜRZBÜCHSEN
Von rechts nach links: Brünn, Mähren, 1872-1922;
Deutschland (?), 19. Jahrhundert; Berlin, frühes 19. Jahrhundert;
Polen, 18.-19. Jahrhundert; Deutschland, 19. Jahrhundert

In Europa wurden turmförmige Gewürzbüchsen, meistens aus Silber, oft zum
rituellen Gewürzriechen am Ausgang des Sabbats benutzt.

הדסים לבשמים
מימין לשמאל: ברנו, מוראביה, 1872-1922; גרמניה (?), המאה הי"ט; ברלין, ראשית המאה הי"ט;
פולין, המאה הי"ח-הי"ט; גרמניה, המאה הי"ט

באירופה נפוץ המנהג להשתמש בכלים דמויי מגדלים, בעיקר מכסף, להרחת הבשמים בטקס ההבדלה
במוצאי שבת.

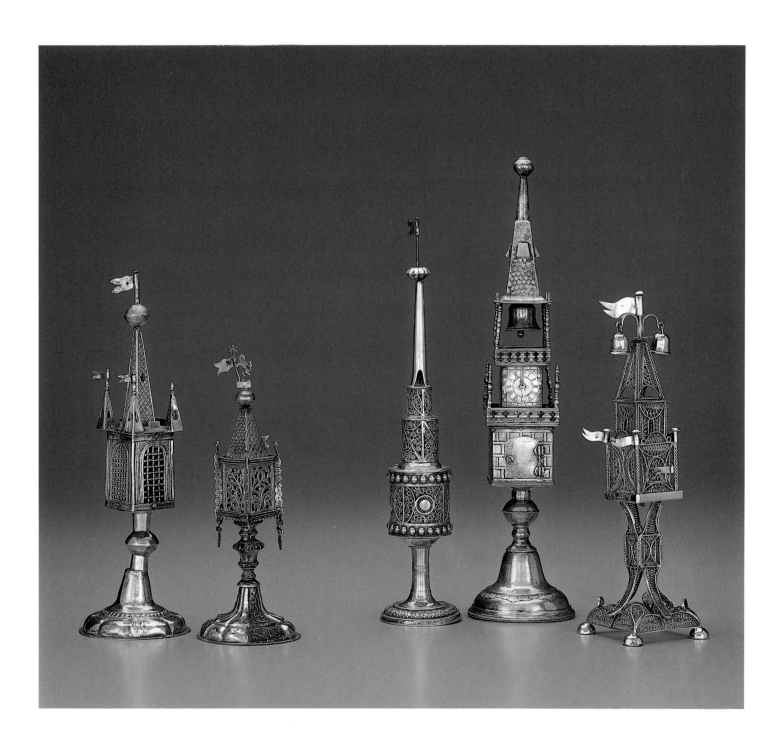

SUKKAH
Fischach, Southern Germany, early 19th century,
painted wood

On the festival of Tabernacles, all meals are served in *sukkot*
(booths). This *sukkah* is painted with both traditional symbolic pictures, including
a depiction of Jerusalem, and genre scenes.

SOUCCAH
Fischach, Allemagne du Sud, début du XIXe siècle,
bois peint

Pendant la fête des Tabernacles les repas sont pris dans des cabanes *(Souccot)*.
Celle-ci est ornée de représentations de sujets symboliques traditionnels
dont une vue de Jérusalem et de scènes de la vie quotidienne.

SUKKAH
Fischach, Süddeutschland, frühes 19. Jahrhundert,
bemaltes Holz

Während der *Sukkoth* Feiertage (Laubhüttenfest) werden
die Mahlzeiten in solchen Hütten eingenommen. Diese *Sukkah* ist mit traditionellen
symbolischen Darstellungen einschließlich einer Ansicht von Jerusalem sowie
mit Genre-Szenen bemalt.

סוכה
פישאך, דרום־גרמניה, ראשית המאה הי״ט. עץ צבוע

הסוכה מקושטת בעיטורים המשלבים סמלים מסורתיים. בהם תיאורי ירושלים מחד גיסא. ומאידך -
בתמונות מחיי יום־יום.

VII

Old Masters and Period Rooms

European civilization represented by paintings, drawings and objets d'art from
the late Renaissance to 19th century Romanticism.
French, Italian and English 18th and 19th century architecture and decorative arts.

Les Vieux Maîtres et les Salles d'Époque

La civilisation européenne d'autrefois représentée par des peintures,
des dessins et des objets d'art depuis la Haute Renaissance jusqu'au romantisme du XIXe siècle.
Architecture et arts décoratifs français, italiens et anglais du XVIIIe et XIXe siècle.

Kunst alter Meister und Stilzimmer

Die Kultur Europas, vertreten durch Gemälde, Zeichnungen und objets d'art von
der späten Renaissance bis zur Romantik des 19. Jahrhunderts. Französische, italienische
und englische Architektur, sowie dekorative Kunst des 18. und 19. Jahrhunderts.

ציורי־מופת וחדרים תקופתיים

תרבות אירופה מיוצגת בציורים, רישומים וחפצי אמנות מסוף תקופת הרנסאנס ועד
הרומנטיציזם של המאה הי״ט. אדריכלות ואמנות דקורטיבית בצרפת, איטליה ואנגליה של המאה הי״ח.

CASKET
Limoges, France, late 16th century,
enamels mounted in gilt copper, h. 12.7 cm

The beautifully preserved translucent enamels, depicting scenes from the
story of Joseph, are possibly by Suzanne de Court.

COFFRET
Limoges, France, fin du XVIe siècle,
émaux sur cuivre doré, h. 12,7 cm

Coffret orné de scènes de la vie de Joseph. Les émaux translucides,
merveilleusement préservés, sont attribués à Suzanne de Court.

KÄSTCHEN
Limoges, Frankreich, spätes 16. Jahrhundert,
Emailarbeit auf vergoldetem Kupfer, H. 12,7 cm

Die schön erhaltenen Emailplatten mit Szenen aus der Josephsgeschichte,
sind möglicherweise von Suzanne de Court gemacht.

תיבת אמאייל
לימוז', צרפת, שלהי המאה הט"ז, ג 12.7 ס"מ

לוחיות האמאייל השקוף, המשובצות בנחושת מוזהבת, נשתמרו להפליא. הן מתארות תמונות מחיי יוסף,
אולי מעשה ידי סוזאן דה קור.

PAOLO DE' MATTEIS, ITALIAN, 1662-1723
The Song of Miriam, oil on canvas, 127 x 180 cm

The artist, a pupil of Luca Giordano, to whom the picture was formerly
attributed, has adopted a composition of his master's.

PAOLO DE MATTEIS, ITALIEN, 1662-1723
Le Chant de Miriam, huile sur toile, 127 x 180 cm

La composition est conçue à la manière de Luca Giordano, le maître de
l'artiste, à qui on avait d'abord attribué cette peinture.

PAOLO DE' MATTEIS, ITALIEN, 1662-1723
Das Lied Miriams, Öl auf Leinwand, 127 x 180 cm

Der Künstler, ein Schüler Luca Giordanos, dem man früher das Bild zuschrieb,
hat hier eine Komposition seines Lehrers übernommen.

פאולו די מאטאיס, איטלקי, 1662-1723
שירת מרים, שמן על בד, 127×180 ס"מ

האמן, מתלמידיו של לוקה ג'ורדאנו - אשר לו יוחסה לפנים התמונה שלפנינו - השתמש כאן
בקומפוזיציה של מורו.

JACOB GERRITSZ CUYP AND AELBERT CUYP, DUTCH,
1594-1651/52 AND 1620-1691
Portrait of a Family in a Landscape, 1641, oil on canvas, 156 x 249 cm
In this key work the figures are by the father Jacob and the landscape by
the young Aelbert.

JACOB GERRITSZ CUYP ET ALBERT CUYP, HOLLANDAIS,
1594-1651/52 ET 1620-1691
Portrait de famille à la campagne, 1641, huile sur toile, 156 x 249 cm
Dans ce tableau remarquable, les personnages sont dus au pinceau de Jacob, le père,
tandis que le paysage a été exécuté par son fils Albert.

JACOB GERRITSZ CUYP UND AELBERT CUYP, HOLLAND,
1594-1651/52 UND 1620-1691
Familienporträt in einer Landschaft, 1641, Öl auf Leinwand, 156 x 249 cm
In diesem Meisterwerk sind die Figuren von Jacob, dem Vater, und die
Landschaft von dem jungen Aelbert gemalt.

יעקב חריטז קייפ ואלברט קייפ, הולנדים, 1594-1651/52 ו־1620-1691
דיוקן משפחה בנוף, 1641, שמן על בד, 156×249 ס"מ

ביצירת־מפתח זו הדמויות הן פרי מכחולו של האב, יעקב, ואילו הנוף צויר בידי הבן, אלברט, בצעירותו.

REMBRANDT VAN RIJN, DUTCH, 1606-1669
The Healing of Tobit, c. 1642-44, pen,
bistre and wash, 9.8 x 13.8 cm

Rembrandt first worked on this motif around 1636. Our drawing is a sketch for a
composition he elaborated upon in several drawings in subsequent years.

REMBRANDT VAN RIJN, HOLLANDAIS, 1606-1669
La Guérison de Tobie, vers 1642-44, plume,
bistre et lavis, 9,8 x 13,8 cm

Rembrandt aborda ce sujet vers 1636. Les années suivantes, il fit plusieurs
ébauches pour sa composition, dont ce dessin.

REMBRANDT VAN RIJN, HOLLAND, 1606-1669
Die Heilung Tobias, um 1642-1644,
Feder und Pinsel, 9,8 x 13,8 cm

Rembrandt behandelte das Thema zuerst um 1636. Diese
Zeichnung ist eine frühe Skizze für eine Komposition, die er in späteren Jahren
in mehreren Versionen entwickelte.

רמברנדט ואן רין, הולנדי, 1606-1669
ריפויו של טוביה, 1642-44 בקירוב, עט, שחמתית ומגוון, 13.8×9.8 ס"מ

רמברנדט החל לעסוק במוטיב זה כבר בסביבות שנת 1636. הרישום שלפנינו הוא מתווה־הכנה
לקומפוזיציה, אשר לקראת ביצועה צייר רישומים אחדים.

JEAN HONORÉ FRAGONARD, FRENCH, 1732-1806
Portrait of the Artist's Father,
red chalk, 25 x 27.8 cm

Establishing eye-contact with the viewer, the merry smile
on the old man's face conceals the agonizing gouty leg and reflects French
18th-century "joie de vivre".

JEAN HONORÉ FRAGONARD, FRANÇAIS, 1732-1806
Portrait du père de l'artiste,
pastel rouge, 25 x 27,8 cm

Le regard communique directement avec le spectateur;
le sourire joyeux dissimule les souffrances du vieillard goutteux et ne révèle
que la joie de vivre bien française de l'époque.

JEAN HONORÉ FRAGONARD, FRANKREICH, 1732-1806
Porträts des Vaters des Künstlers,
Rötel, 25 x 27,8 cm

Das fröhliche Lächeln des alten Mannes, der dem Beobachter sein
Gesicht zuwendet, scheint von dem gichtigen Bein keine Notiz zu nehmen
und spiegelt eher die «joie de vivre» des 18. Jahrhunderts wider.

ז'אן אונורה פראגונאר, צרפתי, 1732-1806
דיוקן אבי האמן, גיר אדום, 27.8×25 ס"מ

נושא הדיוקן יוצר מיד קשר־עין עם המתבונן. ובחיוכו העליז, שכמו בא להסתיר את הייסורים שגורמת
לו רגלו החולה, הוא משקף יפה את רוח שמחת־החיים של צרפת במאה הי"ח.

EIGHTEENTH-CENTURY FRENCH PERIOD ROOM
("The Rothschild Room")

The former "grand salon" of the Hôtel Samuel Bernard,
built c. 1750 at 46 rue du Bac in the Faubourg Saint-Germain in Paris. The
contents, presented together with the room, are of the period.

SALON FRANÇAIS DU XVIIIᵉ SIÈCLE
(«Le Salon Rothschild»)

L'ancien grand salon de l'Hôtel Samuel Bernard au 46 de la rue
du Bac dans le faubourg Saint-Germain à Paris, fut construit vers 1750. La pièce
entière et son contenu sont d'époque.

FRANZÖSISCHES STILZIMMER, 18. JAHRHUNDERT
(«Der Rothschild Salon»)

Der frühere «grand salon» des Hôtel Samuel Bernard, 46 rue du Bac, im Faubourg
Saint-Germain in Paris, wurde um 1750 gebaut.
Die Einrichtung die dem Museum zusammen mit dem Salon gespendet
wurde, stammt aus der gleichen Epoche.

חדר צרפתי מן המאה הי״ח (״חדר רוטשילד״)

ה״סלון הגדול״, לשעבר מבית סמואל ברנאר, שנבנה ב־1750 בקירוב, ברחוב דו באק 46 בפובור־סן־ז׳רמן
בפאריס. תכולת החדר, אשר נתרמה יחד איתו, היא בת התקופה.

EIGHTEENTH-CENTURY ENGLISH DINING ROOM

Pine-panelled room containing period furniture and a collection of eighteenth-century
silver, glass, and porcelain.

SALLE À MANGER ANGLAISE DU XVIIIᵉ SIÈCLE

Chambre lambrissée de pin contenant des meubles et des collections d'argenterie,
verrerie et porcelaine, tous d'époque.

ENGLISCHES ESSZIMMER, 18. JAHRHUNDERT

Der Raum mit Kiefernholz-Täfelung enthält zeitgemäße Stilmöbel und eine
Silber-, Glas- und Porzellansammlung des 18. Jahrhunderts.

חדר אוכל אנגלי, המאה הי״ח

חדר ספון בלוחות אורן, מרוהט ברהיטי התקופה וכולל אוסף חפצי כסף, זכוכית וחרסינה.

74

JEAN-LÉON GÉRÔME, FRENCH, 1824-1904
The Wailing Wall, oil on canvas, 73 x 59.5 cm

This painting is probably based on photographs and drawings made by this Orientalist
artist during a stay in Jerusalem.

JEAN-LÉON GÉRÔME, FRANÇAIS, 1824-1904
Le Mur des Lamentations, huile sur toile, 73 x 59,5 cm

Le tableau a été probablement exécuté d'après des photographies ou des croquis
faits par ce peintre orientaliste lors d'un séjour à Jérusalem.

JEAN-LÉON GÉRÔME, FRANKREICH, 1824-1904
Die Klagemauer, Öl auf Leinwand, 73 x 59,5 cm

Dieses Gemälde wurde wahrscheinlich nach Fotografien und
Zeichnungen gemalt die während eines Aufenthaltes des Künstlers – ein bekannter
Orientalist – in Jerusalem entstanden sind.

ז׳אן־ליאון ז׳רום, צרפתי, 1824-1904
הכותל המערבי, שמן על בד, 73 x 59.5 ס״מ

התמונה מבוססת כנראה על תצלומים ורישומים שנעשו בידי אמן אורייינטליסטי זה בעת שהותו
בירושלים.

VIII

MODERN ART
Impressionism and Post-Impressionism.
Masters of the 20th century.
The School of Paris and early Israeli artists.

L'ART MODERNE
L'impressionnisme et le post-impressionnisme.
Maîtres du XXᵉ siècle.
L'Ecole de Paris et les premiers artistes d'Israël.

MODERNE KUNST
Impressionismus und Post-Impressionismus.
Meister des 20. Jahrhunderts.
Ecole de Paris und Beispiele früher israelischer Kunst.

אמנות חדישה
אימפרסיוניזם ופוסט־אימפרסיוניזם.
אמני המאה העשרים הגדולים. אסכולת פאריס.
אמני ישראל המוקדמים.

PAUL CÉZANNE, FRENCH, 1839-1906
Country House by the Water, 1888-1890,
oil on canvas, 81 x 65 cm

Cézanne painted this landscape in the vicinity of Paris. Beyond
the organization of volume, the artist, rich in experience as a water-colourist,
expressed a deep feeling for nature.

PAUL CÉZANNE, FRANÇAIS, 1839-1906
Villa au bord de l'eau, 1888-1890,
huile sur toile, 81 x 65 cm

Dans ce paysage, peint aux environs de
Paris, Cézanne, riche de son expérience d'aquarelliste, exprime par-delà
l'agencement des volumes, un profond sentiment de la nature.

PAUL CÉZANNE, FRANKREICH, 1839-1906
Landhaus am Wasser, 1888-1890,
Öl auf Leinwand, 81 x 65 cm

An dieser Landschaft, gemalt in der Nähe von Paris,
zeigt Cézanne, mit seiner reichen Erfahrung als Aquarellist, neben der straffen
Strukturierung des Raumes, auch sein tiefes Empfinden für die Natur.

פול סזאן, צרפתי, 1839-1906
בית כפרי על שפת נהר. שמן על בד, 81×65 ס"מ

סזאן, האקוורליסט רב־הנסיון, צייר תמונת נוף זו בקרבת פאריס. מעבר לארגון הנפחים, באה כאן לידי
ביטוי חיבתו העמוקה של האמן לטבע.

PAUL GAUGUIN, FRENCH, 1848-1903
Still Life, 1899, oil on canvas,
44 x 60 cm

An unusual subject for this artist, painted in
the glowing colours of his works done in Tahiti towards the end of his life.

PAUL GAUGUIN, FRANÇAIS, 1848-1903
Nature morte, 1899, huile sur toile,
44 x 60 cm

Sujet peu courant chez l'artiste qui a employé ici la même
palette flamboyante que dans les toiles qu'il a peintes à Tahiti, vers la fin de sa vie.

PAUL GAUGUIN, FRANKREICH, 1848-1903
Stilleben, 1899, Öl auf Leinwand,
44 x 60 cm

Ein ungewöhnliches Thema für diesen Künstler; es zeigt die leuchtenden Farben
der gegen Ende seines Leben in Tahiti gemalten Werke.

פול גוגן, צרפתי, 1848-1903
טבע דומם, 1899, שמן על בד, 60×44 ס"מ

נושא יוצא דופן ביצירתו של האמן, אשר צויר בצבעים הזוהרים המאפיינים את התמונות שצייר
בטאהיטי בשנותיו האחרונות.

EGON SCHIELE, AUSTRIAN, 1890-1918
The City, 1915, oil on canvas, 109.7 x 140 cm

The crowded compressed houses, the
surprising perspective and darkly iridescent colours, endow inanimate objects
with an inner life and reflect the black spirit of war which had engulfed
Europe when this work was painted.

EGON SCHIELE, AUTRICHIEN, 1890-1918
La Ville, 1915, huile sur toile, 109,7 x 140 cm

Les maisons serrées, les unes contre les autres, la perspective
surprenante, et le chatoiement sombre des couleurs semblent insuffler une vie
intérieure aux objets inanimés; la toile est imprégnée de l'humeur noire
de l'Europe plongée dans la guerre à l'époque où ce tableau a été exécuté.

EGON SCHIELE, ÖSTERREICH, 1890-1918
Die Stadt, 1915, Öl auf Leinwand, 109,7 x 140 cm

Die eng gedrängten Häuser, eine überraschende Perspektive und dunkel
leuchtenden Farben geben den unbelebten Objekten inneres Leben und spiegeln
gleichzeitig die düstere Kriegsatmosphäre wider, die in
der Zeit, als das Werk gemalt wurde, Europa umfangen hielt.

אגון שילה, אוסטרי, 1890-1918
העיר, 1915, שמן על בד, 109.7x140 ס"מ

הבתים הצהובים והדחוסים, הפרספקטיבה המפתיעה והצבעוניות הכהה, הזוהרת, מקנים לחפצים
הדוממים חיים משלהם ומשקפים את רוח־הנכאים של המלחמה אשר שרתה על אירופה כאשר צויירה
תמונה זו.

MARC CHAGALL, SCHOOL OF PARIS, BORN 1887
The Rabbi, c. 1914, oil on canvas, 40 x 31 cm

Chagall's Jewish heritage permeates much of the imagery found in his
paintings. This work is one of a number of paintings of praying Jews done in Russia
after the artist's return from Paris and his encounter with Cubism.

MARC CHAGALL, ECOLE DE PARIS, NÉ EN 1887
Le Rabbin, env. 1914, huile sur toile, 40 x 31 cm

L'allégorie dans l'œuvre de Chagall est presque toujours
imprégnée de son héritage juif. Cette toile fait partie d'une série de tableaux de Juifs
en prière peints par Chagall à son retour en Russie, après un séjour
à Paris où il venait de connaître le Cubisme.

MARC CHAGALL, PARISER SCHULE, GEBOREN 1887
Der Rabbi, um 1914, Öl auf Leinwand, 40 x 31 cm

Chagalls jüdisches Erbe findet seinen Ausdruck in einem großen Teil der
Bildersprache seiner Gemälde. Dieses Werk gehört
zu einer Anzahl von Gemälden, die betende Juden darstellen und in Rußland nach
des Künstlers Rückkehr aus Paris und seinem dortigen Zusammentreffen
mit dem Kubismus gemalt worden sind.

מארק שאגאל, אסכולת פאריס, נולד 1887
הרבי, 1914 בקירוב, שמן על בד, 40 × 31 ס"מ

עולם הדימויים של שאגאל ספוג כולו במורשתו היהודית. התמונה שלפנינו היא אחת מקבוצת תמונות
המתארות יהודים מתפללים. היא צויירה ברוסיה לאחר שובו של האמן מפאריס והמפגש עם הקוביזם.

JACQUES LIPCHITZ, SCHOOL OF PARIS, 1891-1973
Musical Instruments, 1918, bronze relief,
56 x 74 cm

This relief, from the Israel Museum's unique
collection of Lipchitz bronzes, reflects the artist's close connection to the
form and subject matter of Cubism in the years 1915-1919.

JACQUES LIPCHITZ, ECOLE DE PARIS, 1891-1973
Instruments de musique, 1918, relief en bronze,
56 x 74 cm

Ce relief fait partie de la collection unique de bronzes de cet artiste appartenant
au Musée d'Israël. Il reflète les rapports étroits que l'artiste a entretenus avec le Cubisme
dans les années 1915-1919, pour ce qui est du sujet et de la forme.

JACQUES LIPCHITZ, PARISER SCHULE, 1891-1973
Musik Instrumente, 1918, Bronzerelief,
56 x 74 cm

Das Relief aus der einzigartigen Sammlung von Lipchitz
Bronzen im Israel Museum, zeigt des Künstlers enge Verbindung mit Form und
Thematik des Kubismus in den Jahren 1915-1919.

ז׳אק ליפשיץ, אסכולת פאריס, 1891-1973
כלי מוסיקה, 1918, תבליט ברונזה, 74x56 ס״מ

תבליט זה שייך לאחת מקבוצות פסלי הברונזה הגדולות של ליפשיץ המצויה באוסף מוזיאון ישראל.
הוא משקף את זיקתו של האמן לעולם הצורות והנושאים של הקוביזם בשנים 1915-1919.

ALEXANDER ARCHIPENKO, BORN RUSSIA, ACTIVE FRANCE, 1887-1964
Woman Combing her Hair, 1914, bronze, 178 x 40 cm

The female figure was Archipenko's prime subject.
The sculpture reflects the influence of Cubism in its optical juxtaposition of interchangeable
concave and convex forms, and in its use of a void to express a mass.

ALEXANDRE ARCHIPENKO, NÉ EN RUSSIE, ACTIF EN FRANCE, 1887-1964
Femme se coiffant, 1914, bronze, 178 x 40 cm

Les femmes étaient le sujet de prédilection d'Archipenko. Cette sculpture reflète
l'influence du Cubisme dans la juxtaposition optique de formes concaves et convexes et dans
l'emploi du vide pour donner l'impression de masse.

ALEXANDER ARCHIPENKO, GEBOREN IN RUSSLAND, ARBEITETE IN FRANKREICH, 1887-1964
Frau ihr Haar kämmend, 1914, Bronze, 178 x 40 cm

Die weibliche Figur war Archipenkos Hauptthema.
Die Skulptur zeigt den Einfluß des Kubismus in ihrer optischen Gegenüberstellung von
auswechselbaren konkaven und konvexen Formen und in ihrer Benützung
der offenen Form eine Masse zum Ausdruck zu bringen.

אלכסנדר ארכיפנקו, נולד ברוסיה, היה פעיל בצרפת, 1964-1887
אשה סורקת שערה, 1914, ברונזה, 178 × 40 ס"מ

דמות האשה היא הנושא הראשי ביצירת ארכיפנקו. הפסל משקף את השפעות הקוביזם במשחק
המתחים בין הצורות המתחלפות מקמורות לקעורות ובניצול החלל לשם ביטוי מאסה.

FERNAND LÉGER, FRENCH, 1881-1955
Composition with Figure, 1924, oil on canvas, 50 x 65 cm

Modern urban and technological culture are embodied
in this work in which the figure and the architecture are strictly regimented to
suggest the metallic yet dynamic qualities of the Machine Age.

FERNAND LÉGER, FRANÇAIS, 1881-1955
Composition, 1924, huile sur toile, 50 x 65 cm

La civilisation urbaine et la technologie moderne sont
incarnées dans cette œuvre. Le personnage et la composition architecturale sont
rigoureusement organisés pour suggérer le
caractère métallique mais aussi le dynamisme de l'ère de la machine.

FERNAND LÉGER, FRANKREICH, 1881-1955
Komposition mit Figur, 1924, Öl auf Leinwand, 50 x 65 cm

In diesem Werk sind moderne urbane und technologische Kultur verkörpert,
wobei Figur und Architektur streng organisiert sind, um auf die metallische und
doch dynamische Qualität des Maschinenzeitalters hinzuweisen.

פרנאן לז'ה, צרפתי, 1881-1955
קומפוזיציה עם דמות, 1924, שמן על בד, 50 × 65 ס"מ

התרבות העירונית והטכנולוגית המודרנית באה לידי ביטוי בתמונה זו. הדמות והפרטים האדריכליים
מאורגנים במשמעת חמורה, כדי להדגיש את האיכויות המתכתיות ועם זה הדינאמיות, המאפיינות את
עידן המכונה.

MARCEL JANCO, ISRAELI, 1895-1984
Bal à Zurich, 1917, oil on canvas, 99 x 101.5 cm

A rare painting from the artist's Dada period in Switzerland. The
painting conveys the ambiance of Zurich cabarets of World War I, including
the "Cabaret Voltaire" where the Dada group was established.

MARCEL JANCO, ISRAÉLIEN, 1895-1984
Bal à Zurich, 1917, huile sur toile, 99 x 101,5 cm

Exécutée en Suisse, c'est une des rares peintures de la période Dada du peintre.
Elle rend bien l'ambiance des cabarets de Zurich pendant
la première guerre mondiale, et en particulier celle du Cabaret Voltaire
où le groupe Dada s'est formé.

MARCEL JANCO, ISRAEL, 1895-1984
Bal à Zurich, 1917, Öl auf Leinwand, 99 x 101,5 cm

Ein seltenes Gemälde aus der Dada-Zeit des Künstlers
in der Schweiz. Das Bild gibt die Stimmung der Zürcher Kabarette zur
Zeit des 1. Weltkrieges wieder, darunter das
«Cabaret Voltaire», mit dem die Dada-Bewegung etabliert wurde.

מרסל ינקו, ישראלי, 1895-1984
נשף בציריך, 1917, שמן על בד, 99 × 101.5 ס"מ

ציור נדיר מתקופת השתייכותו של האמן לקבוצת ה"דאדא" בשווייץ. הוא מעלה את אווירת הקברטים
של ציריך במלחמת העולם הראשונה, ובייחוד "קברה וולטר", שבו נוסדה קבוצת ה"דאדא".

PAUL KLEE, SWISS, 1879-1940
Observations on a Region, 1937, watercolour,
charcoal and chalk ground on newspaper, 48.7 x 32.2 cm

This drawing is an example of Klee's late style and use of humble materials.
His familiar sign language has become stenographic, the lines are heavy and expressive,
and the mood is grave and contemplative.

PAUL KLEE, SUISSE, 1879-1940
Observations sur une région, 1937, aquarelle, fusain et fond
de craie sur papier journal, 48,7 x 32,2 cm

Ce dessin est caractéristique du style tardif de Klee et de l'usage qu'il fit
d'humbles matériaux. Son répertoire de signes familiers est devenu sténographique,
les lignes lourdes et expressives, l'esprit grave et contemplatif.

PAUL KLEE, SCHWEIZ, 1879-1940
Bemerkungen zu einer Gegend, 1937, Aquarell,
Kohle und Kreidegrund auf Zeitungspapier, 48,7 x 32,2 cm

Die Zeichnung zeigt Klees späten Stil und seine Neigung einfache Materialien zu benützen.
Die bekannte Zeichensprache wird mehr und mehr stenographisch,
die Linien sind stark und ausdrucksvoll, die Stimmung ernst und nachdenklich.

פאול קליי, שווייצרי, 1940-1879
הערות על סביבה, 1937, צבעי־מים, פחם ותשתית גיר מעורב בדבק על נייר עיתון 48.7 × 32.2 ס"מ

רישום זה מאפיין את סגנונו המאוחר של קליי, לרבות השימוש בחומרים צנועים. שפת הסימנים המוכרת
שלו הפכה כאן לכתב קצרנות בקווים עבים ועזי־ביטוי ומצב־הרוח הוא רציני ומהורהר.

MAN RAY, UNITED STATES AND FRANCE, 1890-1976
The Mask, 1926,
gelatin silver print, 15.5 x 23 cm

Executed shortly after his arrival in Paris, this photograph
shows the influence of African art and the stylized forms of Brancusi's sculpture
on Man Ray's work at the time.

MAN RAY, ETATS-UNIS ET FRANCE, 1890-1976
Le Masque, 1926,
chloro-bromure d'argent, 15,5 x 23 cm

Exécuté peu après l'arrivée de l'artiste à Paris,
cette photographie est marquée par l'influence de l'art nègre et de la sculpture
stylisée de Brancusi sur l'œuvre de Man Ray à cette époque.

MAN RAY, U.S.A. UND FRANKREICH, 1890-1976
Le Masque (Die Maske), 1926,
Gelatine Silberdruck, 15,5 x 23 cm

Kurz nach der Ankunft des Künstlers in Paris ausgeführt, zeigt
diese Fotografie den Einfluß afrikanischer Kunst sowie den der stilisierten Skulpturen
Brancusis auf Man Rays Arbeiten zu dieser Zeit.

מאןריי, ארה"ב וצרפת, 1890-1976
המסכה, 1926, הדפסי כסף, 15.5 × 23 ס"מ

צילום זה, שצולם זמן קצר לאחר הגיע מאן ריי לפאריס, משקף את השפעת האמנות האפריקאית
והצורות המסוגננות של בראנקוזי על עבודתו באותה עת.

CHAIM SOUTINE, SCHOOL OF PARIS, 1894-1943
Boy in Blue, oil on canvas, 91.2 x 72.5 cm

This painting of an unknown sitter is characteristic of Soutine's
portrait style. The energy-filled brushwork, combined with facial and bodily distortion,
are indicative of the artist's own inner turmoil.

CHAÏM SOUTINE, ECOLE DE PARIS, 1894-1943
Garçonnet en bleu, huile sur toile, 91,2 x 72,5 cm

Cette toile est caractéristique du style des portraits de Soutine.
La touche vibrante d'énergie jointe aux contorsions du visage et du corps de ce modèle
anonyme dénotent l'agitation intérieure de l'artiste.

CHAIM SOUTINE, PARISER SCHULE, 1894-1943
Junge in Blau, Öl auf Leinwand, 91,2 x 72,5 cm

Diese Gemälde eines unbekannten Modells ist charakteristisch für Soutines Porträt-Stil.
Die energiegeladene Pinselarbeit sowie die Gesichts-
und Körperverzerrungen, zeigen des Künstlers innere Unruhe.

חיים סוטין, אסכולת פאריס, 1894−1943
נער בכחול, שמן על בד, 72.5×91.2 ס"מ

ציור זה של עלם אלמוני אופייני לסגנון הדיוקנאות של סוטין. משיכות־המכחול הנמרצות, יחד עם
עיוותי הפנים והגוף, מעידים על הסערה הפנימית בנפשו של האמן.

YOSSEF ZARITSKY, ISRAELI, BORN 1891
Safed, c. 1924, water-colour over black chalk, 63 x 61 cm

The dramatic semi-abstract vision of the old Galilean town is an early work
of a remarkable water-colourist.

YOSSEF ZARITSKY, ISRAÉLIEN, NÉ EN 1891
Safed, env. 1924, aquarelle sur craie noire, 63 x 61 cm

Cette vision dramatique, quasi abstraite, de cette très ancienne ville de Galilée est
l'œuvre d'un admirable aquarelliste à ses débuts.

YOSSEF ZARITSKY, ISRAEL, 1891
Safed, um 1924, Aquarell über schwarzer Kohle, 63 x 61 cm

Die dramatische halb-abstrakte Vision der alten galiläischen Stadt, Safed, ist ein
Frühwerk des bedeutenden Aquarellisten.

יוסף זריצקי, ישראלי, נולד 1891
צפת, 1924 בקירוב, צבעי-מים על-גבי גיר שחור, 63 × 61 ס"מ

תיאור דרמאטי מופשט-למחצה זה של העיר הגלילית הוא מיצירותיו המוקדמות של זריצקי,
האקוורליסט המעולה.

87

IX

CONTEMPORARY ART

The growing collection of international and Israeli art:
painting, drawing, sculpture, photography and design after 1945.

L'ART CONTEMPORAIN

Développement de la collection d'art international et israélien:
peinture, dessin, sculpture, photographie et
design après 1945.

ZEITGENÖSSISCHE KUNST

Wachsende Sammlungen internationaler und israelischer Kunst:
Malerei, Graphik und Skulpturen, Photographie
und Design nach 1945.

אמנות בת־זמננו
האוסף ההולך וגדל של אמנות בינלאומית וישראלית.
ציור, רישום, פיסול, צילום ועיצוב
אחרי 1945.

ANNA TICHO, ISRAELI, 1894-1980
Jerusalem Hills, 1975, charcoal and pastels,
50.5 x 74.5 cm, signed and dated 1975

The monumental landscape of the Judaean Hills which surround the city of Jerusalem
constituted Anna Ticho's favourite subject throughout her life.

ANNA TICHO, ISRAÉLIENNE, 1894-1980
Les Collines de Jérusalem, 1975,
fusain et pastel, 50,5 x 74,5 cm

Le panorama monumental des collines de Judée tout autour de Jérusalem a été
le sujet de prédilection d'Anna Ticho tout au long de sa vie.

ANNA TICHO, ISRAEL, 1894-1980
Jerusalemer Berge, 1975, Kreide und Pastellfarben,
50,5 x 74,5 cm, signiert und dated 1975

Die monumentale Landschaft der Judäischen Berge der Umgebung Jerusalems stand
während ihres ganzen Lebens im Mittelpunkt von Anna Tichos Werk.

אנה טיכו, ישראלית, 1894-1980
הרי ירושלים, 1975, פחם ופסטל, 50.5 × 74.5 ס"מ, חתום ומתוארך 1975

נוף ירושלים, על הריה הצחיחים, היה הנושא החביב על אנה טיכו במרוצת כל שנות חייה.

PABLO PICASSO, SPANISH, 1881-1973
Seated Woman, 1949, oil on canvas, 100 x 81 cm

Women were always an important source of inspiration in Picasso's art,
and they are present in all of his many stylistic periods. This portrait reflects his
preoccupation with a specific, flat, stylized pattern.

PABLO PICASSO, ESPAGNOL, 1881-1973
Femme assise, 1949, huile sur toile, 100 x 81 cm

Les femmes ont été une source d'inspiration inépuisable dans l'art
de Picasso. Il les a peintes dans tous les styles. Dans ce portrait datant de 1949, on sent
l'intention d'aboutir à une forme stylisée, sans relief.

PABLO PICASSO, SPANIEN, 1881-1973
Sitzende Frau, 1949, Öl auf Leinwand, 100 x 81 cm

Frauen waren immer eine wichtige Inspiration in Picassos Kunst und sie erscheinen
in Werken der verschiedensten Stilarten. Dieses Porträt von 1949
spiegelt seine Versuche wider mit einem flachen stilisierten Muster zu arbeiten.

פאבלו פיקאסו, ספרדי, 1881-1973
אשה יושבת, 1949, שמן על בד, 100 × 81 ס"מ

נשים היו מאז ומתמיד מקור השראה חשוב באמנותו של פיקאסו ונוכחותן בולטת בכל הסגנונות הרבים
שבהם יצר. דייקן זה מבטא את התעניינותו בדגם מסוים, שטוח ומסוגנן.

HENRY MOORE, BRITISH, BORN 1898
Vertebrae, 1968, bronze, 355 x 710 x 355 cm

The sculpture is based on the overlap of internal and external forms. The work exudes
a feeling of movement and the parts suggest a coupling and intermingling of limbs.

HENRY MOORE, ANGLAIS, NÉ EN 1898
Vertèbres, 1968, bronze, 355 x 710 x 355 cm

La sculpture, composée d'éléments concaves et convexes, donne une impression
de mouvement permanent, évoquant des membres entrelacés.

HENRY MOORE, ENGLAND, GEBOREN 1898
Vertebrae, 1968, Bronze, 355 x 710 x 355 cm

Die Komposition basiert auf dem Ineinandergreifen von inneren und äußeren Formen.
Es entsteht ein Gefühl von Bewegung, wobei die einzelnen Teile
an ineinander verflochtene und verschlungene Gliedmaßen erinnern.

הנרי מור, בריטי, נולד 1898
חוליות, 1968, ברונזה, 355 × 710 × 355 ס"מ

התפיסה הצורנית של פסל זה מתבססת על חפיפה של צורות חיצוניות ופנימיות. הפסל מעורר תחושה
של תנועה וחלקיו מרמזים על אברים משתרגים ומתמזגים זה בזה.

JEAN TINGUELY, SWISS, BORN 1925
XK^3, 1965, painted iron, 400 x 287 x 97.5 cm

The sculpture, a combination of wheels, transmission belts and various
metal parts painted black, reminiscent of 19th-century machines, moves by electricity
and charms us with its craftsmanship and irony.

JEAN TINGUELY, SUISSE, NÉ EN 1925
XK̃^{3}, 1965, fer peint, 400 x 287 x 97,5 cm

Cet assemblage de roues, courroies de transmission, pièces de métal,
actionné par l'électricité, rappelle les machines du XIXe siècle. On est séduit par
son côté artisanal où se mêle une pointe d'ironie.

JEAN TINGUELY, SCHWEIZ, GEBOREN 1925
XK̃^{3}, 1965, bemaltes Eisen, 400 x 287 x 97,5 cm

Die elektrisch betriebene Skulptur, eine Kombination von Rädern, Treibriemen und
verschiedenen Metallteilen, schwarz bemalt, erinnert an
Maschinen des 19. Jahrhunderts. Ihre handwerkliche Qualität, gemischt
mit leichter Ironie, ist höchst reizvoll.

ז׳אן טינגלי, שווייצרי, נולד 1925
XK3, 1965, ברזל צבוע, 400 × 287 × 97.5 ס"מ

הפסל, המורכב ממערכת גלגלים, רצועות תמסורת וחלקי מתכת שונים צבועים בשחור, ונע בכוח
החשמל, מזכיר מכונות מן המאה הקודמת ומעורר את חיבתנו באומנות הרכבתו ובאירוניה שבו.

Jean Dubuffet, French, born 1901
Logologie, 1974, vinyl on panel, 217 x 320 cm

In Dubuffet's *Hourloupe* series (1962-1975) the forms originate from a
sort of doodling and the colour is reduced to the black, red and blue of felt
tip markers. In *Logologie* all reference to real things is abolished.

Jean Dubuffet, Français, né en 1901
Logologie, 1974, vinyl sur bois, 217 x 320 cm

Dans la série *Hourloupe* de Dubuffet (1962-1975), les formes émergent
d'une libre écriture; les couleurs sont limitées au noir, rouge et bleu des crayons
feutres. Dans *Logologie* toute référence aux choses réelles est supprimée.

Jean Dubuffet, Frankreich, geboren 1901
Logologie, 1974, Vinyl auf Holz, 217 x 320 cm

In Dubuffets *Hourloupe*-Serie (1962-1975) entstehen die Formen aus einer Art von
«doodling», wobei die Farbe auf das Schwarz, Rot und Blau von Filzstiften reduziert ist.
In *Logologie* wird jeglicher Bezug auf «wirkliche Dinge» vermieden.

ז׳אן דובופה, צרפתי, נולד 1901
לוגולוגיה, 1974, ויניל על לוח, 217 × 320 ס״מ

בסדרה "אורלופ" של דובופה (1962-1975) נובעות הצורות מתוך מעין שרבוט והצבעוניות מצטמצמת
לשחור, אדום וכחול של עטי-לבד. ב"לוגולוגיה" נעדרת כל התייחסות שהיא לעצמים מציאותיים.

ARIE AROCH, ISRAELI, 1908-1974
The High Commissioner, oil on wood panel, 116 x 73 cm

Aroch discovered this image of the British High Commissioner in Palestine on a popular wall-hanging. The image, the core of the painting, controls the sophisticated interaction between the components of the composition.

ARIÉ AROCH, ISRAÉLIEN, 1908-1974
Le Haut-Commissaire, huile sur bois, 116 x 73 cm

Aroch découvrit cette image du haut-commissaire britannique en Palestine sur un tapis. L'image, qui est l'essentiel du tableau, contrôle l'action mutuelle des éléments de la composition.

ARIE AROCH, ISRAEL, 1908-1974
Der Hochkommissar, Öl auf Holz, 116 x 73 cm

Aroch entdeckte dieses Bildnis des Britischen Hochkommissars in Palästina auf einem volkstümlichen Wandbehang. Das Bildnis, das den Kern des Gemäldes ausmacht, kontrolliert das geistreiche Zusammenspiel zwischen den einzelnen Teilen der Komposition.

אריה ארוך, ישראלי, 1974-1908
הנציב העליון. שמן על לוח עץ. 116 × 73 ס"מ

את דימוי הנציב העליון הבריטי בארץ-ישראל מצא ארוך על-גבי שטיח-קיר עממי. דימוי זה הפך בציור לגרעינה של הקומפוזיציה, והוא מכתיב את יחסי-הגומלין המתוחכמים שבין מרכיביה.

MENASHE KADISHMAN, ISRAELI, BORN 1932
Suspense, 1966, painted iron, 302 x 228 x 39 cm

The artist uses strong simple shapes, painted in brilliant primary yellow, to create
a contrasting effect against the landscape background.

MENASHÉ KADISHMAN, ISRAÉLIEN, NÉ EN 1932
Suspense, 1966, fer peint, 302 x 228 x 39 cm

L'artiste choisit des formes simples qu'il peint en jaune
primaire éclatant, pour qu'elles se détachent bien sur la toile de fond du paysage.

MENASHE KADISHMAN, ISRAEL, BORN 1932
Spannung, 1966, bemaltes Eisen, 302 x 228 x 39 cm

Der Künstler benützt starke einfache Formen, die in leuchtendem
Primargelb gemalt sind um einen kontrastierenden Effekt gegen den Hintergrund
der Landschaft hervorzurufen.

מנשה קדישמן, ישראלי, נולד 1932
מתח, 1966, ברזל צבוע, 302 × 228 × 39 ס״מ

האמן השתמש בצורות פשוטות, חזקות, צבועות בצבע צהוב בסיסי זוהר, כדי ליצור אפקט של ניגוד
ביחס לנוף המהווה רקע לפסל.

MOSHE KUPFERMAN, ISRAELI, BORN 1926
Painting, 1972, oil on canvas, 99.5 x 115.5 cm

A restrained and austere painting, based on the tension between a decisive linear
structure and a painterly surface.

MOSHE KUPFERMAN, ISRAÉLIEN, NÉ EN 1926
Peinture, 1972, huile sur toile, 99,5 x 115,5 cm

Peinture réservée et austère, basée sur la tension entre la structure linéaire
et le plan pictural.

MOSHE KUPFERMAN, ISRAEL, GEBOREN 1926
Gemälde, 1972, Öl auf Leinwand, 99,5 x 115,5 cm

Ein zurückhaltendes und strenges Gemälde,
dessen Wirkung auf der Spannung zwischen klar begrenzter linearer Struktur
und malerischer Oberfläche beruht.

משה קופפרמן, ישראלי, נולד 1926
ציור, 1972, שמן על בד, 99.5 × 115.5 ס"מ

ציור חמור ומאופק, המתבסס על המתח שבין מבנה קווי מודגש לפני שטח "ציוריים".

DAVID SMITH, AMERICAN, 1906-1965
Cubi VI, 1963, stainless steel, 285 x 73 x 54 cm

Smith's Cubis (twenty-eight in number) form his last series of sculptures and are
regarded as among the artist's greatest works.

DAVID SMITH, AMÉRICAIN, 1906-1965
Cubi VI, 1963, acier inoxydable, 285 x 73 x 54 cm

Les Cubis, au nombre de vingt-huit, forment la dernière série de sculptures de l'artiste.
Ils sont considérés comme ses œuvres les plus remarquables.

DAVID SMITH, U.S.A., 1906-1965
Cubi VI, 1963, rostfreier Stahl, 285 x 73 x 54 cm

Die Reihen der Cubis – es gibt im ganzen 28 – sind die letzten Skulpturen des
Künstlers und werden zu seinen besten Werken gezählt.

דייוויד סמית, אמריקאי, 1906-1965
קובי VI, 1963, פלדת אל־חלד, 285 x 73 x 54 ס"מ

סדרת ה"קובים" של סמית (28 עבודות) היא סדרת הפסלים האחרונה שיצר, והיא נחשבת בין עבודותיו
המעולות.

ANDY WARHOL, AMERICAN, BORN 1931
Golda Meir, 1975,
silkscreen and acrylic paint on canvas, 101 x 101 cm

It is not so much Warhol's choice of image so much as its presentation that
makes the painting so provocative. The directness of the
original photograph, transformed into the silkscreen, is heightened by
touches of colour applied with a brush.

ANDY WARHOL, AMÉRICAIN, NÉ EN 1931
Golda Meïr, 1975,
sérigraphie et acrylique sur toile, 101 x 101 cm

Ce n'est pas tant le choix de l'image que sa présentation qui rend cette
peinture si provocante. L'effet immédiat de la photographie originale, transformée
en sérigraphie, est rehaussé par des touches de couleur
appliquées au pinceau.

ANDY WARHOL, U.S.A., GEBOREN 1931
Golda Meir, 1975,
Siebdruck und Acrylfarben auf Leinwand, 101 x 101 cm

Es ist weniger Warhols Wahl des Themas als vielmehr die Art
der Darstellung die das Bild so provokativ macht. Die Unmittelbarkeit der Fotografie
übertragen auf Siebdruck, wird durch mit dem Pinsel aufgetragene
Farbflecken verstärkt.

אנדי וורהול, אמריקאי, נולד 1931
גולדה מאיר, 1975, הדפסי־משי וצבע אקריליק על בד, 101 × 101 ס"מ

נימתו המתגרה של הציור מושגת לאו דווקא על־ידי בחירת הנושא אלא על־ידי אופן הצגתו. תחושת
המיידיות והישירות שמשרה התצלום מוגברת מכוח משיכות־המכחול הצבעוניות.

R.B. KITAJ, BORN USA 1932, RESIDES ENGLAND
Self-portrait in Saragossa, 1980,
pastel and charcoal on paper, 147.3 x 85.1 cm

A unique self-portrait conveying an overpowering sense of emotional stress
and dissonance.

R.B. KITAJ, NÉ AUX ÉTATS-UNIS EN 1932, RÉSIDE EN ANGLETERRE
Autoportrait à Saragosse, 1980,
pastel et fusain sur papier, 147,3 x 85,1 cm

Un autoportrait incomparable qui communique une impression envahissante de
dissonance et de tension émotionnelle.

R.B. KITAJ, GEBOREN 1932 IN DEN U.S.A., LEBT IN ENGLAND
Selbstporträt in Saragossa, 1980,
Pastell und Kohle auf Papier, 147,3 x 85,1 cm

Ein einzigartiges Selbstporträt, das ein überwältigendes Gefühl von emotioneller
Spannung und Dissonanz vermittelt.

ר״ב קיטאי, נולד בארה״ב ב-1932, מתגורר באנגליה
דיוקן עצמי בסראגוסה, 1980. פסטל ופחם על נייר, 147.3 × 85.1 ס״מ

דיוקן עצמי מיוחד במינו, המעורר תחושה עזה של חוסר-הארמוניה ומצוקה נפשית.

AVIGDOR ARIKHA, ISRAELI, BORN 1929
Going Out, 1981, oil on canvas, 87 x 71 cm

In recent years, Arikha has specialized in painting which is an accurate
rendition of reality. Here the imposing and meticulous composition gives a sense of
timelessness to the depicted moment.

AVIGDOR ARIKHA, ISRAÉLIEN, NÉ EN 1929
Sortie, 1981, huile sur toile, 87 x 71 cm

Arikha s'est engagé, ces dernières années, dans une peinture
qui reproduit fidèlement la réalité. L'organisation imposante et méticuleuse de cette
composition donne l'impression que l'instant est fixé sur la toile pour l'éternité.

AVIGDOR ARIKHA, ISRAEL, GEBOREN 1929
Vor dem Ausgehen, 1981, Öl auf Leinwand, 87 x 71 cm

In den letzten Jahren hat Arikha sich in seiner Malerei auf klare Wiedergabe
der Realität spezialisiert. In diesem Werk gibt die
imponierende und genau gegliederte Komposition dem dargestellten
Augenblick ein Gefühl von Zeitlosigkeit.

אביגדור אריכא, ישראלי, נולד 1929
לקראת היציאה, 1981, שמן על בד, 87 × 71 ס"מ

בשנים האחרונות מתמחה אריכא בציור המתאר באופן מדויק את המציאות. בציור שלפנינו מקנה
הקומפוזיציה החמורה, הבנויה בקפידה, ממד של על־זמניות לרגע המתואר.

CHILDREN'S PAINTING OF THE OLD CITY OF JERUSALEM
Pastel on black paper, 1979

Group project by twelve-year-old children participating in one of the hundred art classes
offered weekly by the Israel Museum's Youth Wing and the Paley Art Center.

LA VIEILLE VILLE DE JÉRUSALEM PEINTE PAR DES ENFANTS
Pastel sur papier noir, 1979

Travail de groupe exécuté par des enfants de douze ans qui
assistent à l'un des cent cours d'art qu'offre le Musée d'Israël au Pavillon des Jeunes
«Ruth» et au Centre Artistique Paley.

KINDERZEICHNUNG DER JERUSALEMER ALTSTADT
Pastell auf schwarzem Papier, 1979

Gruppenarbeit von 12-jährigen Kindern die an einem der hundert
wöchentlichen Kursen teilnehmen die das Israel Museum im «Ruth» Jugendmuseum
und im Paley Kunstzentrum bietet.

העיר העתיקה, ציור ילדים
צבעי פסטל על נייר שחור, 1979

יצירה קבוצתית של ילדים בני שתים-עשרה המשתתפים באחת ממאה הכיתות לאמנות
אשר מתקיימות מדי שבוע באגף הנוער ע"ש רות במוזיאון ישראל ובמרכז פיילי לאמנות.

WILLEM SANDBERG, DUTCH, 1897-1984
New Buildings in Old Environments, 1979,
poster, 68 x 68 cm

The exhibition for which Sandberg created this photo-collage
presented architectural solutions to the problem of integrating new buildings into old,
or even ancient, surroundings.

WILLEM SANDBERG, HOLLANDAIS, 1897-1984
Edifices nouveaux, environnements anciens, 1979,
affiche, 68 x 68 cm

L'exposition pour laquelle Sandberg a créé ce photo-collage,
présentait des solutions architecturales au problème de l'intégration heureuse de
bâtiments nouveaux dans des environnements anciens, voire antiques.

WILLEM SANDBERG, HOLLAND, 1897-1984
Neue Gebäude in alten Umgebungen, 1979,
Poster, 68 x 68 cm

Die Ausstellung, für die Sandberg diese Photo-Collage geschaffen hat,
zeigte architektonische Lösungen zu dem Problem der erfolgreichen Eingliederung
moderner Gebäude in historischen Umgebungen.

וילם סנדברג, הולנדי, 1897-1984
בניינים חדשים בסביבות ישנות, 1979, כרזה, 68 x 68 ס"מ

התערוכה אשר למענה יצר סנדברג קולאז׳־צילומי זה הציגה פתרונות אדריכליים לבעיה כיצד לשלב
בניינים חדשים בתוך סביבה של בתים ישנים, או אפילו עתיקים.

TABLE OF CONTENTS AND PROVENANCE OF OBJECTS

CREDITS

Editorial Consultant: Yona Fischer
Managing Editor: Irène Lewitt
Photography: Pierre-Alain Ferrazzini, Geneva
Photography Coordinator: Genya Markon
Design: Pierre-Alain Ferrazzini, Geneva and Jean Genoud, Lausanne
Hebrew typography: Ora Yafeh
Producer: Offset-litho Jean Genoud SA, Lausanne, Switzerland
Hebrew typesetting: Ben-Zvi Enterprises Ltd., Jerusalem
Binder: Mayer et Soutter, Lausanne, Switzerland

Published 1985 by The Israel Museum, Jerusalem

Printed in Switzerland
First Printing 1985